THE GREEK SENSE OF THEATRE

THE GREEK SENSE OF
THEATRE

TRAGEDY REVIEWED

I

J. Michael Walton

METHUEN
LONDON AND NEW YORK

First published in 1984 by
Methuen & Co. Ltd
11 New Fetter Lane, London EC4P 4EE
Published in the USA by
Methuen & Co.
in association with Methuen, Inc.
733 Third Avenue, New York, NY 10017

© 1984 J. Michael Walton

Printed in Great Britain at
the University Press, Cambridge

British Library Cataloguing in Publication Data

Walton, J. Michael
The Greek sense of theatre.
1. Theatre - Greece
2. Greek drama (Tragedy) - History and criticism
I. Title
882'.01'09   PA3201

ISBN 0-416-36710-0
ISBN 0-416-36720-8 Pbk

Library of Congress Cataloging in Publication Data

Walton, J. Michael, 1939-
The Greek sense of theatre.
Includes index.
1. Theater - Greece
2. Greek drama (Tragedy) - History and criticism
I. Title
PA3201.W349 1984   792'.0938   84-14725

ISBN 0-416-36710-0
ISBN 0-416-36720-8 (pbk.)

FOR SUSAN

CONTENTS

ILLUSTRATIONS

ACKNOWLEDGEMENTS

The extracts from *The Republic of Plato* are from the translation by F.M. Cornford (1941) and are reprinted by permission of Oxford University Press. The passage from Aristotle's *Politics* is copyright to the estate of T.A. Sinclair (© 1962), and reprinted by permission of Penguin Books Ltd. Unless otherwise stated translations from the Greek are the author's.

The cover illustration is based on a bas-relief figure of Hecuba, one of Fifteen Figures of Greek Drama by Edward Gordon Craig (Florence, 1908), by kind permission of Robert Craig and the Edward Gordon Craig estate.

PROLOGUE

There is a translation of a Euripides play which has a messenger entering with the words: 'Oh, Oh. Oh. Gloomy news.' It is a line to raise the temperature and lower the resistance, to soften the resolve and harden the artery. My heart goes out to all messengers with gloomy news, actors who have to play them, audiences who have to listen to them. It encapsulates, I fear, a common experience in the face of Greek tragedy on page or stage, having all the crowd-pushing appeal of a lecture I once attended on 'Some hitherto unexplored aspects of Turkish puppetry'.

Greek tragedy was an art form born two and a half thousand years ago from a culture whose values and concerns are no longer familiar. But because the playwrights were engaged in dramatizing human experience, because the gods and heroes who peopled the stage were 'examples' as well as characters, because the theatre of the Athenians was a place where ideas were translated into art, it is still possible, given favourable circumstances, for Greek drama to be seen as both alive and immediate. Reading the plays in a sensitive translation can be a rich experience, seeing them performed something far more. Tragedy need not be gloomy news.

By comparison with the other arts of the Greek world, drama is in a healthier position than music, knowledge of which is reduced to the titles of a number of differing 'modes' to be played on various wind, string or percussion instruments. On the other hand, it is disadvantaged by comparison with painting, sculpture and architecture, which assorted mutilations have diminished without incapacitating. Dance is in a similar position to drama. We have access to plenty of written material in strict verse in response to which dancers danced. A number of vase-paintings from the sixth century BC onwards show men and women dancing. A lot but a little. The problem is similar for tragedy.

Greek tragedy survives in a small but presumably representative selection of texts, backed by a minimum of verifiable facts about the various features of performance. To many people that would appear to be sufficient. But no one would consider that we can get much notion of Greek dance from reading an Aeschylean chorus. Dance is understood as a performance art. Too often drama is not.

The Greek theatre was a performance medium which incorporated drama, dance and music. The inadequate state of our knowledge of the nature of that performance does not rule out the value of re-appraising what does survive, to see if the dramatic texts may include a sense of the theatre and its possibilities, which, as working playmakers and practitioners, the Athenian tragedians understood and explored.

The survival of the plays, few as they are, has ensured that they have over the years received the best of attention from literary critics. The canon of Attic tragedy stands alone until the Middle Ages in providing an understanding of the art of drama alongside the arts of sculpture, painting, music and literature. It is always with the last of these that drama has been most closely linked. Because the plays are available most readily in print, the page is often regarded as the most suitable place for them. There the literary and many of the dramatic qualities can be sifted and scrutinized.

The theatrical qualities, by which the plays can be seen to be performance pieces, are less commonly stressed, partly because performance is so difficult to recreate and partly because the visual aspect of the Greek theatre has for so long taken second place to the spoken word. For all the valuable work of Lillian Lawler, Oliver Taplin and most recently, David Seale, it is still the common belief that what was *said* in the Greek tragedies was more important than what was *seen*. It was not so, I would maintain, for the Athenians of the fifth century BC. The actor may have been *hupokrites*, an 'answerer' or 'expounder of a story', but the *choros* was a chorus of dancers who performed in an *orchestra*, not a place for musicians as in English usage, but a dancing-place. The action of the play was a '*drama*', 'something done', not 'something spoken', and the spectators, *theatai*, sat, not in an auditorium, a 'hearing-place', but in a *theatron*, a 'seeing-place'. The Greeks went to the theatre to witness a performance. The implications of this are too often ignored, even by the theatre historian. J.L. Styan represents the majority voice when he writes of the root of the word 'theatre': 'the act of seeing was not at the heart of this occasion, we can be sure, and the absence of visual detail in Greek tragedy supports this'.[1] I hope to show that we cannot be sure; that there is no lack of visual detail in Greek tragedy; and that the theatre of the Athenians was one of the more spectacularly visual in the history of the drama.

The further back one goes towards the time when epic was first transformed into dramatic, the clearer it is that early tragedy was always some sort of a spectacle, whatever Aristotle had to say about it two hundred years later. Even he believed it to have developed from the dithyramb, a dance for a chorus of fifty participants.

In translation Aeschylus, the first playwright some of whose work survives, seems the wordiest of the tragedians because so much of his expression is difficult to understand. What I hope to show is that this difficulty arises from too close and too literal a concern with the words alone. A consideration of even the small number of Aeschylus' texts shows that he crafted his plays fully aware of the medium in which he was working and of which he was the master. Aeschylus was not only a writer. He was, we are told, his own choreographer, designer, perhaps composer and certainly first actor.

It is customary, even in such a visual age as our own, for theatricality to be dismissed in academic circles as sheer trickery, used to gloss over difficult ideas or even as a substitute for them. But at its best the theatrical offers a means of opening

---

1 *Drama, Stage and Audience*, Cambridge, Cambridge University Press, 1975, p. 111.

up a story or an argument, of augmenting intellect with emotion and understanding. The great playwrights of the world's stage have been distinguished by fine minds and fine sensibilities. They have not always, as Arthur Miller once pointed out, been fine writers. He went on to argue that this did not matter because playwrights reveal their ideas to audiences through the whole language of the theatre, a language in which words are often less telling than sound and in which the stage picture often says more in a single pause than through a page of dialogue. The world of Aeschylus, Sophocles and Euripides is a world in which objects speak volumes, where the silent character can show himself more powerful than the speaker and the movement of a dozen men in masks can give a living embodiment to the hopes and fears of an entire community.

It is my belief that the audience in Athens were quite capable, even those among them who could not read the printed word, of reading those artistic signals which form the language of the stage as one of the links between themselves, the world about them, their fellow men and their gods. The fifth century BC saw the flourishing and the decline in Athens of a civilization which was built around the visual arts. It was the age of the architect, the painter and the playwright. Only in the fourth century did these forms decline in favour of an emphasis on the spoken word. Then the historians, the philosophers and the rhetoricians kept Athens a centre of intellectual pursuit. And the theatre became an actor's theatre. Picture gave way to speech.

This may well imply that there was a decline from physical performance in the theatre as the fifth century reached its closing years. In all probability the commonplace sentiments of Euripides' heroes and heroines did require a more fluid and less formal presentation for the subtleties of their sentiments to reach even a proportion of the huge audiences. Playwrights usually directed their own plays and it is possible to see how Aeschylus, Sophocles and Euripides too, individually and in different ways, reinforced the most basic of stories with layer upon layer of extra meaning. Though no later tragedies survive from which a proper comparison can be made, it does seem by inference that what the later playwrights lacked was the ability to employ the concrete language of the stage. When drama became the province of the star actor, the thematic image became subordinate to the flamboyant ego.

This book does not profess to be a comprehensive study of the Greek theatre or its tragic drama. Some of the world's greatest plays are summed up and 'dealt with' in a few pages with barely one aspect considered. Nor has my intention been to offer a formula to a modern director for staging Greek tragedy. What I hope I have done is draw attention to a particular element in the making of plays, which I believe to have been uppermost in the minds of the practitioners, but which has often been neglected because of the demands of classical scholarship. The Greeks made no use of stage-directions, at least in the written texts as they have been transmitted to the modern reader. There is no body of contemporary criticism to help us 'see' the performances as the first audiences saw them. And there is no manual of stagecraft to give definitive advice on the form and conventions of Greek theatre.

Even if it is not possible to make up for these deficiencies, it must at least be worth demonstrating that such a lack does not disinherit modern readers and audiences from those works which first suggested a universal theatre aesthetic. When first presented the plays were accessible to a far larger proportion of the population than has visited the theatre at any time since. Though it would be fanciful to imply that in Greek tragedy may be found some key to restoring the theatre as part of a community's consciousness, any study of the drama which fails to take this 'popularity' into account is only helping to relegate the plays to shelves. Greek tragedy is not of the museum, even a museum of theatre. It belongs on the stage, renewed and invigorated by an informed generation of actors, designers and directors.

PART I
THE ATHENIANS
AND THEIR THEATRE

1

THE CRITIC

STAGE DIRECTOR: The first dramatist understood what the
modern dramatist does not yet understand. He knew that
when he and his fellows appeared in front of them the
audience would be more eager to *see* what he would do
than to *hear* what he might say. He knew that the eye is
more swiftly and powerfully appealed to than any other
sense; that it is without question the keenest sense of the
body of man. The first thing which he encountered on
appearing before them was many pairs of eyes, eager and
hungry. Even the men and women sitting so far from him
that they would not always be able to hear what he might
say, seemed quite close to him by reason of the piercing
keenness of their questioning eyes. To these, and all, he
spoke either in poetry or prose, but always in action: in
poetic action which is dance, or in prose action which is
gesture. (Edward Gordon Craig, 1905)[1]

Aeschylus was that first dramatist, and it is one of the theatre's
greater losses that Craig never directed a production of any of
his plays. He did create a number of designs for Eleanora Duse
as Electra in Hofmannsthal's adaptation of the Sophocles play,
but, as with so much of his work, this got no further than some

1 *The Art of the Theatre*, London and Edinburgh, T.N. Foulis, 1905, pp. 20-1.

startlingly effective drawings. The most famous has the down-
cast figure of Electra with arms outstretched, silhouetted in the
foreground against the massive verticals of a doorway upstage.
On the steps before the door huddle an indecisive group whose
shrinking inaction complements and focuses Electra herself.
He also made a series of bas-relief black figures, no more than a
few inches high, Hecuba among them, in which he concentrated extreme emotion as is found in the outline of the masked
performer. In an earlier passage from *The Art of the Theatre*
Craig claims the dancer rather than the poet as 'father of the
dramatist'. His remarkable vision of the theatre at a time when
the stage was struggling into the twentieth century away from
both melodrama and naturalism, found more detractors than
converts at the time of writing; his evocation of 'the theatre of
the ancients', as he called it, even less sympathy within formal
classical scholarship.

As a point of aesthetics, the relationship between the aural
and the visual had been the subject of discourse for centuries
among philosophers and theoreticians. Even Horace suggested
to the budding playwrights of Augustus' time to whom the *Ars
Poetica* is addressed that the eye is a more 'trustworthy agency'
than the ear, and warned them thereby to be careful about what
they showed on stage. Lessing in the *Laocoon* (1766) described
stoicism as basically undramatic, maintaining that strong emotions should be displayed rather than talked about. And though
he asserted that the poet is not compelled, as is the sculptor, 'to
concentrate his description into the space of a single moment',
his comprehension of the overlap between artistic forms allows
for the complex image that links the theatrical tableau to the
sculpture.

Schiller too, in the preface to *The Bride of Messina* (1803),
commended the idea of the chorus for 'disturbing the illusion'
and castigated the French neo-classicists 'who have utterly
misconceived the spirit of the ancients'. And Schiller it was
who made one of the strongest professions of the theatre's sin-
gularity when he wrote: 'In dramatic works what is desired is
illusion, which, if it could be accomplished by means of the
actual, would be, at best, a paltry illusion. All the externals of a
theatrical representation are opposed to this notion; all is
merely a symbol of the real.'

Yet somehow the prevailing view handed down has been that

Greek drama was language: Greek tragedy, 'of course presents itself to us only as word-drama', as Nietzsche has it in *The Birth of Tragedy* (1872). But this is absurd. The Greek theatre represented a fusion of art forms allied to a specific and unique theatrical quality. The fact that a majority of classical scholars have overlooked this quality in favour of excessive emphasis on the spoken word can be attributed to two factors. The first is that the performance details for the fifth century BC are meagre. The second factor is that, despite Schiller, too much attention has been paid to Aristotle, who, in the *Politics* and the *Poetics*, appeared to downgrade all such aspects of the theatre. In this chapter I wish to consider the *Poetics*, the founding document of European dramatic theory, and account for the emphasis Aristotle placed on dramatic construction at the expense of theatrical values. This emphasis has, I believe, distorted our view of the tragedians of the classical era.

It is hardly the fault of Aeschylus, Sophocles or Euripides that so few of the physical conditions within the Greek theatre have been handed down to us. They created their plays for a single performance with little, if any, expectation of a second, and only a slim chance of subsequent publication. We have to turn to others to discover what the Greeks thought about their theatre, notably to Aristotle, the first 'critic' of the ancient world. But if Aristotle was the first critic, it is wise to recall that he was writing seventy years after the deaths of Sophocles and Euripides. His claim to the title comes by default. The fifth century BC did not number among its preoccupations the need to capture the present for the sake of the future. Herodotus of Halicarnassus and Thucydides did record aspects of the recent and not-so-recent past for specific purposes, but neither paid more than passing attention to day-to-day affairs in Athens. It was simply not in the brief they set themselves. For any impression of the texture of Athenian life in the fifth century we must turn, not to historians, but to the comic playwright Aristophanes and the philosopher Plato. Neither had the writing of social history as an aim; both give away details in passing of public and private concerns and activities. And both had things to say about the theatre. In the absence of any criticism in the modern sense, we can at least gain some impression of how fifth-century Athenians evaluated the theatre of their own time. So different, both Aristophanes and Plato serve to put Aristotle in perspective.

Aristophanes was a comedian. His plays acknowledge the theatre and glory in its ways. He includes references to the audience, to the settings and to stage machinery which are helpful in recreating both the atmosphere and the details of old comedy. He introduces contemporary figures as characters and, if satire is usually at the expense of veracity, the presence of a stage Socrates or Euripides is a tribute to their notoriety. Aristophanes produced *Frogs* at the Lenaia of 405 BC, only months after the deaths of both Sophocles and Euripides. Dionysus, god of the theatre, has decided to try and bring back Euripides from Hades to save the dramatic festivals. Arriving on the other side of the river Styx, he discovers that there is no general agreement that Euripides would be the best candidate for resurrection. Dionysus decides to hold a competition between Aeschylus, dead over fifty years, and Euripides for the 'chair' of drama. The competition consists of the two playwrights – Sophocles, who probably died inconveniently with the play already written and in rehearsal, is virtually ignored – making fun of one another's work and defending their own.

The whole contest is farcical, of course, and the conclusion, which finds Aeschylus rather than Euripides returning to Athens, is the result of political rather than dramatic factors. However, Aristophanes does offer an insight into the style of the two playwrights. In the absence of any alternative view, what is said in the competition has perhaps assumed more weight than it merits, the 'weight' of lines being a major factor by which Aeschylus is regarded as superior to Euripides. One issue in passing does point towards an important truth.

Euripides complains, among other things, about Aeschylus' use of the silent figure, sitting with face covered in aspect of grief, saying nothing, while the chorus 'sets about a cluster of odes'. Aeschylus defends himself and later accuses Euripides of reducing tragedy by the use of unsuitable characters and unsuitable costumes, the often-quoted 'kings in rags'. These sallies are no more than minor aspects of a battle which rages over prologues, over language, over theme and character. Alone they could hardly be used as evidence of the primacy of theatrical elements in the plays. What is important, however, is the admission by Aristophanes, through his characters, of aspects of the theatre that can only be implied from the scripts. Such references give licence to search out a technique of play-making that takes account of and, indeed, trades upon such notions as tableau, contrast and stage picture, not as a modern way of viewing ancient plays, but as a part and parcel of the theatre from the beginning.

The Aeschylus and Euripides of *Frogs* are presumably as fictional as the Aristophanes of Plato's *Symposium*, who can offer no contribution at first to the discussion of the nature of love because of hiccups. He subsequently founds his theory on the belief that man was originally a double being, who was cut in two for his wickedness and condemned to pine for the missing half. The fable serves as light relief for the dinner guests before Socrates contributes a more serious consideration. To a great extent both Socrates and Aristophanes are Plato speaking.

The same is true of the characters in the *Republic*, in which Plato offers his formidable opposition to drama and the theatre. The *Republic* is a lengthy treatise in dialogue form on the nature of justice. Early on a number of minor characters offer definitions of justice. Socrates finds each in turn wanting and suggests that it may be easier to approach such an abstract subject by considering first the ideal city-state. After some discussion this is agreed to be made up of three classes, guardians, soldiers and workers, analogous to elements within mankind, as long as these classes are able to work in perfect harmony. Socrates proceeds to consider the education of the guardian or philosopher class and expounds the Platonic 'Theory of Forms'. It is from this theory that all his reservations about drama stem.

As expounded in the *Republic* the Theory of Forms assumes that everything on this earth is an imitation or pale reflection of its *form*. At one level the *form* of man is God. Physical objects also have *forms* and the chair on which you sit, or the table at which you eat, is itself an imitation of the *form* of chair or table. The *forms* contain within themselves all that contributes to the excellence in any chair or table.

Such a severe doctrine imposes moral problems for the educationalist. Poetry was for the Athenian as much a part of education as reading, writing or physical exercise, but in the 'ideal state' it must be the right kind of poetry. Fiction, Socrates argues, means 'telling lies'. Homer, by presenting gods who cheat and steal, is doubly telling lies. Any dramatic poetry which deals with the gods in a less than favourable light is similarly suspect and should be excluded from the curriculum. Similar logic is applied to the presentation of a child dishonouring a parent or a hero fearing death. As a result almost any situation occurring in the surviving tragedies and comedies turns out to meet, through the eyes of the characters, with Plato's disapproval.

As if this were not enough, the disputants next attack the actor. By a process of strict, if untenable, logic, we are shown that it must be bad for a good man to deviate from his own character to show the audience a bad man. Bad men must not be copied. By a further argument it is agreed that a man can only do one thing best and Socrates is led to the following conclusion:

> Here then, Adeimantus, is a question for you to consider: Do we want our Guardians to be capable of playing many parts? Perhaps the answer follows from our earlier principle that a man can only do one thing well; if he tries his hand at several, he will fail to make his mark in any of them. Does not that principle apply to acting? The same man cannot act many parts so well as he can act one.
> No, he cannot.
> Then he will hardly be able to pursue some worthy occupation and at the same time represent a variety of different characters. Even in the case of two forms of representation so closely allied as tragedy and comedy, the same poet cannot write both with equal success. Again, the recitation of epic poetry and acting on the stage are distinct professions; and even on the stage different actors perform in tragedy and comedy.
> That is so.
> (*The Republic of Plato*, III, 394–5, trans. F.M. Cornford, Oxford, Oxford University Press, 1941)

It follows that if a man can represent a bad character on stage without shame, then he cannot be a good man. Why? Because if he were a good man he would not know how to behave as a bad man. Socrates concludes:

> Suppose, then, that an individual clever enough to assume any character and give imitations of anything and everything should visit our country and offer to perform his compositions,

we shall bow down before a being with such miraculous
powers of giving pleasure; but we shall tell him that we are
not allowed to have any such person in our commonwealth.

(ibid., III, 397)

So the theatre is to be excluded from the 'ideal state'. But the
reasons for its exclusion, though overlapping with the reservations against poetry, are here identified in the person and nature
of the actor. Theatre *is* considered as performance and it is that
special nature which makes it, for Plato, so dangerous.

Later, drama comes under attack when Socrates attempts to
compose a theory of art. Tragedy is distinguished from epic by
mimesis, 'representation'. Here as in other art forms, such as
sculpture and painting, artistic achievement is to be judged by
likeness to life. Poet and painter imitate life, so that artistic
creation is at one remove from life: hence second-best. But life
itself is, by the Theory of Forms, only second-best to start with.
Dramatic representation is twice removed from 'reality'. This
makes it only third-best and the *Republic* has no use for the
third-best.

On one further occasion Socrates and his friends tangle with
the theatre when, late on in the *Republic*, the moral effect of
poetry becomes the subject of debate and tragedy is pilloried for
exciting in the audience emotions which ought to be kept in
check:

Can it be right that the spectacle of a man behaving as one
would scorn and blush to behave oneself should be admired
and enjoyed, instead of filling us with disgust?
No, it really does not seem reasonable.
It does not, if you reflect that the poet ministers to the satis-
faction of that very part of our nature whose instinctive
hunger to have its fill of tears and lamentations is forcibly
restrained in the case of our own misfortunes.

(ibid., X, 605–6)

It is this last point, the effect on the audience, which was of
most concern to Aristotle. To the theatre historian his *Poetics*
is almost more trouble than it is worth. For all that he provided
the substance from which the theorists and practitioners of the
Renaissance fashioned their theatrical revival, Aristotle was
principally a philosopher. To be more accurate, he was, perhaps,

the first of the polymaths. Living in an age when most 'know-ledge' could be known by the same man, he wrote extensive works on natural philosophy, ethics, politics and rhetoric among a reputed output of some four hundred works. His philo-sophy provides a general standpoint for all his writing and any comments either he or Plato made about drama need to be con-sidered in this perspective.

Aristotle studied for twenty years under Plato. The *Poetics* was written as a direct challenge to his mentor: a philosophical refutation of Plato's theory of Art, a re-examination of the con-cept of *mimesis* and a declaration in favour of the emotional impact of dramatic performance. Aristotle inherits from Plato and accepts the Theory of Forms and does not take issue with the idea that dramatic poetry is at least one step from reality. But when he does take issue with his master, he writes as a philosopher in answer to a philosopher with specific ideas to refute.

All of which makes many aspects of the *Poetics* easier to understand, even if it fails to account for the reverence with which every word was treated for so many hundreds of years. It does go some way to explain why there is so little reference to the chorus in the *Poetics*, why the presentation of plays is vir-tually ignored and why the only person in classical Athens who might have witnessed revivals of the tragedies as a critic, when those plays were no more than a generation old, gives little impression of them as stage pieces. That aspect does not feature in his argument.

The organization of material as we have it in the *Poetics* is fairly haphazard. It is thought to have been a series of lecture notes and unrevised. Certainly Aristotle promises in the *Poli-tics* to explain things in the *Poetics*, which he simply never gets round to in the text we have. Even were it a finished work, it was not intended by its author to be a commentary on theatre past, still less a manual for future playwrights. If the details Aristotle does include of the growth and development of tragedy and comedy sound vague, the dramatic criticism nebulous, so they are, being no more than staging-posts on a philosophical journey.

Though Aristotle clearly did not set out to write a history of the theatre, he found it necessary to reiterate some of the assumptions of his own day about how tragedy and comedy were born. Clearly he had information available to him which has not survived for us. Though much of this could have been hearsay evidence, it would have included complete written records of victors in the dramatic competitions, which have only come down to us in truncated form. He would also have had the festival performances of his own day. Plays were still performed in Aristotle's time in the Theatre of Dionysus during the festivals of the Lenaia and the Great Dionysia. Indeed the first permanent stone facade built by Lycurgus dates from about the same time as the *Poetics*. The programmes at these two main festivals and at a host of minor local festivals frequently featured revivals of the works of the fifth-century BC masters in a period when the craft of play-making was in decline, but the actor had come into his own. Surely with the apparent proximity in time to the works of Aeschylus, Sophocles and Euripides, it would be rash to challenge any of Aristotle's beliefs about even the earliest Athenian theatre.

A quick glance at the relatively few sections of the *Poetics* which pass comment on the development of theatre in Greece confirms not only that the questions which have taxed generations of later scholars interest Aristotle only marginally, but that he acknowledges his lack of comprehensive data. His lack of concern in historical matters is a direct result of his overriding purpose in writing the *Poetics* in the first place.

The Ionian logographers had provided a transition from the epic poems to the specialized histories of Herodotus, Thucydides and Xenophon, but in Aristotle's time, the past of even two hundred years previously was decidedly hazy. Archaeological discoveries, comparative cultural research and historical perspective have put the modern historian in at least as strong a position to unearth the social and religious life of early Athens as that of the host of writers of the Hellenistic and Roman periods whose own versions of history are so wayward and contradictory.

Anthropological theories on the origins of tragedy which relate it to symbolic battles between dark and light, the ritualized celebration of the agrarian calendar or the religious invocation of dead heroes, all relate plausibly to the earliest manifestations of a dramatic form in almost any organized society. The derivation of the word 'drama' from the verb *dran*, 'to do', is sufficiently vague for the term to encompass all manner of dances and cryptodramatic response from the solemn stamping of Aboriginal Mudmen to the gnashings of the enchanted *Barong* or the conscious mysticism of Pueblo Indian rites. These are dramas, fettered neither by outside convention nor by the spoken word, subject only to the religious bond of performer/priest and audience/participants. Such forms have been traced back over two millennia before the birth of Aeschylus and can still inspire a sense of awe, however diluted their modern manifestations.

As the various cities of Greece emerged from their dark ages it would have been unusual had they not promoted aspects of civic ritual into some kind of dramatic form. That some of these forms should have been comic is less surprising than that the comic and solemn should have developed in different ways. That they should have been fortified by the secular tradition of the travelling entertainer, be he bard, clown or contortionist, reflects nothing more revolutionary than the tendency to absorb and codify social practice typical of a community growing from a hand-to-mouth existence into full civic order.

Such a secular tradition is more than hinted at in Homer, for whom the bard is a figure of significance in the community. From his approach to his material, from his performance and from the response of his audience, the Homeric bard is clearly a forerunner of the actor. What prevents him from being an actor is the simple difference between telling a story and *mimesis* or 'imitation'. The story-teller commentates on a conversation from the distance of the third person – 'He said ''. . .'', but she replied ''. . .'' ' – and fills in between passages of dialogue with linking narrative. So performed the Homeric bard, and so the oral tradition by means of which Homer was transmitted to the Athenians until the first standardized text was commissioned by Pisistratus for the Great Dionysia.

Later historians and grammarians, though significantly Aristotle never mentions him in the *Poetics*, understood Thespis to have 'invented' acting. The dates are unclear, but, if Thespis existed at all, 532 BC seems the most reliable date for the first performance of a tragedy. But what does it mean to say he 'invented' acting? It seems to be clear enough that the contribution of the first actor was simply to 'become' by *mimesis* the characters whose speech he had previously catalogued. This is certainly the process which Plato found to be so damaging to

the individuals concerned. Description is assimilated into dialogue, epic becomes dramatic and bard becomes actor.

The transition is straightforward enough, but there is a more
important implication for the nature of Greek drama, though
one that must needs be more speculative. In the *Odyssey* it is
not unusual for the bard to be joined by a chorus of dancers who ✓
perform with him, apparently to give emphasis to his story. The
implications of that relationship will be considered in chapter
4. The importance of dance as an element in the drama is
emphasized by Aristotle in the opening section of the *Poetics*
when he refers to the way in which dancers 'arrange the
rhythms of their movements to represent men's characters and
feelings'. He later asserts that tragedy developed from
'improvisation' and from the dithyramb, a cyclic dance for fifty
performers, featured in competition on festival occasions. The
common belief is that the chorus was originally the whole
drama, but that the chorus leader emerged as an independent
actor. I hope to show later that chorus and the actor may always
have been independent, as were bard and chorus; that the
chorus served to provide a visual dimension to the actor, at least
in earliest times; and that the development of Greek tragedy
should be seen less as a simple evolution from choral to actor
drama, than as a complex means of exploring the possibilities
afforded by the varying relationships among all the performers.

Tragedy was specifically Athenian. Athens produced the only
three tragedians whose work has survived and we know by
name a whole host of lesser lights. When Aristotle tells us that
both tragedy and comedy were originally 'improvisation', he
uses the adjective *autoschediastike*, the precise meaning of
which is not clear. *Autoschediastikos* does not seem to describe
unscripted dramatic situations where the outcome is uncertain
until the performance and where the actors are expected to
react spontaneously in character. It may mean the kind of
highly rehearsed and developed acting technique found in the
Commedia dell' Arte, in which the actors possess a basic store
of situations, jokes and responses and adapt them to a given
scenario. This might provide a further link through to the bard
or epic reciter, who appears to have had a similar stock of
descriptive passages, epithets and rhythmic 'fillers' within
which to frame his latest work.

If Aristotle knew about Thespis as the 'inventor' of acting or

of tragedy, he must have included him within his, for us,
regrettably casual 'The successive stages through which
tragedy passed and the authors of these changes are not
unknown'. Failure to relate the dramatic to epic more directly
as a performance art may be unfortunate but can hardly be
considered an omission. Instead, Aristotle does offer some
passing remarks on the relegation of the chorus in favour of
dialogue, the raising of the number of actors to two by
Aeschylus and three by Sophocles, who is also said to have
introduced scenic decoration.

Details of staging practice are clearly of no interest to
Aristotle and are included under the blanket title of *opsis*. Every
tragedy, he concludes, has six elements which determine its
quality: plot, character, diction, thought, *opsis* and music.
Opsis is usually translated 'spectacle', but effectively covers
the entire visual dimension which I suggest was of prime
importance in tragedy. Clearly, if the only writer to concern
himself with the drama chooses to relegate the visual to the
fifth of six elements, some explanation is called for, particularly as only a little later Aristotle adds, after due consideration
of the first four elements, that music is perhaps the most important of the remaining embellishments, *opsis* having an emotional appeal, but being the least skilful element and least the
province of the creative artist: 'For the power of tragedy can be
felt without production or actors, while the handling of scenic
effects is more the responsibility of the stage-manager
(*skeuopoios*) than the poet'.

Aristotle notably fails here to make a necessary distinction
between production externals and the manner in which a
playwright employs them. For all Aristotle must be assumed to
have attended the dramatic festivals in Athens, he never writes
like a theatre-goer. He does make mention of actors of the classical period who were critical of one another or were themselves criticized for extravagance, but from Aristotle alone one
can get no impression whatsoever of what performances in
either his own or any previous period actually looked like.
Indeed he confesses that as far as he is concerned, it is quite
possible to get as much from a tragedy by reading it as by seeing
it, an attitude given unfortunate authority by later generations.

Inevitably the chorus means virtually nothing to Aristotle:
'They should be regarded as one of the actors'. He records that

Agathon, who is also given credit for the brief introduction of the 'fictional' plot, was the first to reduce the chorus to an interlude in the drama, as it is in the texts of the comedies of Menander first produced just before Aristotle's death in 322 BC. He gives little impression of the music which accompanied the lyrics nor of the substantial dance element. Almost all such aspects of performance are downgraded by Aristotle and are, as he admits, of less interest to him than plot, character, diction and thought. Aristotle makes tragedy seem a literary and private art form. This does not give us authority to consider the classical theatre in the same way.

The most important philosophical assumption that Aristotle inherits from Plato concerns the term *mimesis*. Though the basis of the actor's art, Aristotle uses it in a Platonic sense. In the *Republic*, *mimesis* is used to refer not only to 'imitation' or 'dramatic representation', but also in the sense of a 'copy'. The arts, music, dance and drama are assumed to be 'copies' of reality. Art is thus defined in imitative terms explained by man's natural feeling for rhythm and melody and his innate instinct for 'imitation' (*mimesis*). It is against this inherited notion of art as 'imitation' in the sense of 'copy' that one must regard the Aristotelian rules, rules of dramatic structure onto which Renaissance writers latched and which dominated French classicism. By far the most significant of these were the three Unities – of time, of place and of action.

When Aristotle first differentiates between epic and dramatic, he considers metrical structure, then the narrative nature of epic and adds, 'They differ again in length: for tragedy endeavours, as far as possible, to confine itself to a single revolution of the sun, or but slightly to exceed this limit; whereas the epic action has no limits of time'. This is the only reference in the *Poetics* to the Unity of time. It is tentative at best and as applied to the surviving tragedies is virtually irrelevant.

In no surviving fifth-century play does the playwright seem to have subscribed to such a habit, never mind rule, with the possible exception of Sophocles' *Ajax*, the plot of which hinges on a prophecy that the hero will overcome his difficulties if he can only live through the present day. As applied elsewhere, the recommendation is nothing more than an acknowledgement by Aristotle that a playwright would be ill-advised to try and dramatize the whole of the *Iliad* or the *Odyssey* at one time. Where so many critics have misled themselves is in assuming that it makes any difference to the *Oresteia* whether Agamemnon arrives home an hour, a day or a week after Clytemnestra sees the beacon which announces the fall of Troy. It is none of these periods of time. It is simply one scene later.

In a later section on the differences between epic poetry and tragedy Aristotle amplifies his earlier remarks on the scope of the subject matter of each by pointing out, 'In tragedy we cannot imitate several actions carried on at one and the same time. We must confine ourselves to the action on the stage and the part taken by the players'. This is the only reference in the *Poetics* to the Unity of place. Again Aristotle is doing no more than point out a fairly obvious aspect of dramatic structure in his own time, namely that it was not possible to show scenes running concurrently. Epic poetry can do this. And the staging practice of later times has allowed both for simultaneous setting and the juxtaposition of brief scenes to demonstrate synchronicity.

Aristotle does not say here or anywhere else that a play must have a single setting. Most Greek tragedies do. Aeschylus' *Eumenides* and Sophocles' *Ajax* do not. In a theatre which employed such splendid devices as the *mechane* and the *ekkuklema*, changes of location were seldom necessary. When the playwrights did need them they used them. That the audiences might have found the breaking of the Unity of place disconcerting seems untenable within a tragic tradition which ran in tandem with the comic tradition of old comedy. Aristophanes moves his characters from earth to heaven, down to Hades via the river Styx and even into a city in mid-air without ever, it would seem, straining the audience's sense of stage convention.

The Unity of action merits slightly more serious consideration if only because the term is sufficiently imprecise to encompass comic interlude, sub-plot and consistency of character. Again for philosophical rather than aesthetic reasons, Aristotle is concerned with the scope of a single tragedy. The Unity of action requires only that the action be complete in itself and so arranged that no part could be displaced or removed without damaging the whole. As with the Unities of time and place, so with the Unity of action Aristotle argues for little more than that a play should be decently constructed. Greek tragedy is anyway notoriously difficult to cut even for an audience unversed in its conventions and structure. Part of the reason is the sheer economy of the classical tragedians. Unexpected scenes, such as the arrival of the Nurse in the *Libation-Bearers* of Aeschylus or the argument between Admetus and his father in Euripides' *Alcestis*, are never irrelevant to the plot. Similarly, the apparent overstatement of Orestes' and Electra's long lament or Admetus' self-recrimination in the same plays turns out to be of major consequence.

Consciously or unconsciously the major tragedians did subscribe to the Unity of action. The same cannot be said for the Unities of time or place. Indeed I doubt if anything more lay behind Aristotle's remarks upon them than simple observation of the more successful tragedies of his own and former days. That he used the construction of such plays to justify the value of tragedy and epic in the education of the young is a different matter, one that ties in finally with the emotional impact of tragedy in action.

Aristotle's main argument in the *Poetics* is centred on the famous definition of tragedy. This is worth repeating in full because it directly relates a sense of theatre to its effect:

> Tragedy, then, is an imitation of an action that is serious, complete, and of a certain magnitude; in language embellished with each kind of artistic ornament, the several kinds being found in separate parts of the play; in the form of action, not of narrative; through pity and fear effecting the proper purgation of these emotions. By 'language embellished', I mean language into which rhythm, 'harmony', and song enter. By 'the several kinds in separate parts', I mean that some parts are rendered through the medium of verse alone, others again with the aid of song. (Aristotle, *Poetics*, VI, 2–3, trans. S.H. Butcher, London, Macmillan, 1895)

The translation is a little stilted, but any translation of this celebrated passage needs glossing because of the terms Aristotle uses.

'Imitation' is *mimesis*, used by both Aristotle and Plato in the dual sense of a 'reflection of reality' or a 'copy' and of the act of 'assuming a character'. In this single word is highlighted one of the central differences between Plato and Aristotle. Plato argued that we become like what we imitate. Hence the art of acting was morally damaging principally for the actor, though

also for the audience. Aristotle neutralizes *mimesis* by introducing a new notion of tragic art.

'Action', *praxis*, is not so much stage action and the for-
warding of the plot as a composite accomplishment of a set of
given circumstances. The second time the word 'action' is
used, 'in the form of action, not of narrative', Aristotle uses a
different Greek word from *praxis*, *dronton* being the genitive
plural of the present participle of *dran*, 'to do'. Though it is
difficult to render the difference in English, a more suitable
translation might read 'through doing things rather than
talking about them'. The contrast being made is again between
the dramatic and the epic, *dran* being the root verb of *drama* and
dramatikos.

Spoudaios, here translated 'serious', means more 'worth
taking seriously'. 'Complete' and 'of certain magnitude' are
fair translations of terms explained in detail in the ensuing
argument about the appropriate length and scope of tragedy.

Lastly there is 'the proper purgation', the regular translation
of *katharsis* until the direct transliteration established itself in
the critical vocabulary. Aristotle first referred to 'catharsis' in
the *Politics*:

> We accept the classification of melodies as given by some
> educationalists – ethical, active, and emotional, and regard
> the harmonies as being appropriate one here and another
> there in that scheme. But we say that music ought to be used
> not as conferring one benefit only but many; for example, for
> education and cathartic purposes (here I use the term
> 'catharsis' without further qualifications; I will treat of it
> more fully in my work on *Poetics*), as an intellectual
> pastime, as relaxation and for relief after tension. . . . Any
> feeling which comes strongly to some exists in all others to a
> greater or less degree, pity and fear, for example, but also this
> 'enthusiasm'. This is a kind of excitement which affects
> some people very strongly. It may arise out of religious
> music, and it is noticeable that when they have been listen-
> ing to melodies that have an orgiastic effect they are, as it
> were, set on their feet, as if they had undergone a curative
> and purifying treatment. And those who feel pity or fear or
> other emotions must be affected in just the same way to the
> extent that the emotion comes upon each. To them all comes
> a pleasant feeling of purgation and relief. In the same way

cathartic music brings men an elation which is not at all harmful. Hence these are the harmonies and melodies that ought to receive particular attention from those who are concerned with contests in theatrical music.

In the theatre there are two types of audience, the one consisting of well-educated gentlemen, the other of common persons, drawn from the menial occupations, paid workers and such-like. For the relaxation of this latter class also competitions and spectacles must be provided. But as their minds have become distorted, removed from the condition of nature, so also there are deviations from the norm in their harmonies, in the unnatural pitch and tone of their melodies. Each group finds pleasure in that which is akin to its nature. Therefore allowances must be made for theatrical producers when they use the type of music that appeals to this class of audience.

(Aristotle, *Politics*, VIII, 7, trans. T.A. Sinclair, Harmondsworth, Penguin, 1962)

This is a long quotation but so revealing, not least for its elitism, that it saves much speculation about Aristotle's use of 'catharsis' in the *Poetics*. 'Catharsis' has become almost a synonym for 'recreation'. Plato had admitted the need for recreation in order to restore the emotional balance. Aristotle allows the theatre this recreational function and welcomes, with suitable safeguards, a theatre which can deeply affect its audience.

It is only the effect on the spectator, as the *Politics* shows us, which is at issue here. Literally *katharsis* means a 'cleansing' or 'purification'. It is a religious as well as a medical term. After Orestes has killed his mother, for example, he is required to perform certain cathartic rites. These do not free him from the attentions of the Furies but they do fulfil his immediate religious obligations.

In this theatrical context Aristotle seems to identify 'catharsis' in one of two ways. It happens, he suggests, that in all of us there exists a certain potential for emotion. The value of the religious/dramatic festival, and of tragedy in particular, is that it excites this emotion, or rather these emotions identified as 'pity' and 'fear' and exorcises them. The audience feels sympathy with the stage characters and achieves a release of emotional tension by weeping on their behalf. Or to reduce the

argument from the sublime, we would be entitled to think that
Aristotle might have applauded the sentiment of Ogden Nash
that

Virtue's noble and Vice is vile
But you need an orgy once in a while.

The theatre as orgy, then: or perhaps, as an experience, the
watching of tragedy is a kind of spiritual emetic, contributing
actively to the sanity and balance of individual and community.

An alternative view of the definition is to consider that
Aristotle thinks of the emotions much as he does the muscles of
the body. As under-used parts of the body will become flabby or
even atrophy, so our emotional muscles need to be kept in trim,
even by proxy, for when we need them. Such an idea may well
fit an aesthetic theory of the function of theatre, but the passage
from the *Politics* quoted above would appear to indicate that
Aristotle understood 'catharsis' in the former sense.

What we have, then, is a succinct, if occasionally ambiguous,
justification for the theatre and, in particular, for tragedy in the
community. So succinct indeed was Aristotle's account of dramatic 'engagement' that is was not seriously challenged until
Piscator and Brecht in our own century.

If I have here stressed the reasons for the *Poetics* being
written in the form it was, it is principally in order to demonstrate why it should not be treated as a playwriting manual.
Still less, I would suggest, is it a fair commentary on the theatre, either of Aristotle's own time or of the fifth century BC
when most of the plays which he uses as examples were
written. I talk of 'the theatre' rather than 'the drama' because it
is only through Aristotle's insight into audience response that
we are given any real indication of the classical theatre as a
living performance art. Aristotle is not at fault in this. We
merely need to approach the *Poetics* with caution. When
Aristotle writes that plot is more important than character, he
writes as a philosopher and not as a dramatic critic. He may be
correct with regard to the drama of the classical period, if not
necessarily our own. He is still ordering his priorities as part of a
larger argument.

When he places *opsis* and *melopoia*, 'spectacle' and 'song', as
the last of the six elements of drama, it is not good grounds for

suggesting that Aeschylus, Sophocles and Euripides relegated
them in the same manner. Aristotle does say that a plot should
be constructed which will excite pity and fear 'without seeing',
but his argument is for a drama that is not merely extravagant.
He puts his remarks in proper perspective when he indicates a
little later that the playwright 'in constructing the plot. . .
should place the scene before his eyes', and even work it out
'with the gestures (*schemasin*) in mind'.

It appears to be Aristotle's impression that this was the way
that the great tragedians of the fifth century BC had worked, and
here we can breathe a sigh of relief. At last he is referring to the
elements of theatre about which this book is written. We can
look now at those people for whom the plays were really created,
the Athenian audiences, to see how their understanding of the
theatre may have affected the playwrights.

2
THE PLAYGOERS

Details of the original performances being largely a battle-ground for scholars, the Greek tragedies have tended to remain on the page, aloof from the rest of the world's repertoire. Secure in their authority as corner-stones of European literature they have only occasionally been subject, as are dramatic corner-stones, to the interested sniff of the passing director. Paradoxically this makes Greek tragedy vulnerable to generalization. Everybody knows a little about it, nobody a lot.

The most common of these generalizations concerns the religious aspect of the plays. Critics of the older school, when they thought of performance at all, chose to consider it as a kind of ritual. The more recent critics disavow this, pointing to the lack of direct association between the plays and the festivals at which they were performed. Yet the view persists that the performance of tragedy and comedy in Athens at festivals in honour of a god is in itself proof that a fifth century BC audience responded to the works of Aeschylus, Sophocles and Euripides as though they were attending, if not a twentieth-century church service, at least a medieval mass. It is not so much that the modern age falls into the Victorian trap of viewing Olympian morality through Christian spectacles, but rather that post-Nietzschean scepticism finds it hard to accept that those otherwise advanced and thoughtful dramatists really believed in their gods. If they did take them seriously, the argument proceeds, then Aeschylus and Sophocles must surely have accorded to the gods they introduced into their plays a supernatural authority, while Euripides clearly introduced gods onto his stage in order to prove that they did not exist at all.

Greek tragedy, I would suggest, contains no such general affirmations of faith, or lack of it. Still less does it indicate that, even during the seventy years when the three major tragedians flourished, there was a static and universal body of religious belief. The theatre was a place for the dissemination of ideas and all the playwrights took advantage of the structure of myth to consider the relationships between the natural and supernatural worlds. This relationship is a study in itself, but a single element of it is relevant to an understanding of the Greek sense of theatre.

The Greek saw himself in relation to the world around him, a world which existed for his benefit, but left him at the mercy of a number of contrary and unpredictable forces. His sense of the past and his sense of art were both dominated by a limited number of gods cast in his own image, but a host of minor powers and exceedingly large abstracts such as Fate and Necessity had the controlling interest in his life. It was a world of signs and omens, if you knew how to read them, a world in which objects had significance and skills an almost tangible value.

The theatre was a place in which to contemplate the vicissitudes of life and seek guidance over major issues. It was also a place in which those forces which controlled life outside could be assimilated through the agency of actors promoted by the stage to heroes and gods. On that stage nothing stood in isolation. Background, setting, costume, mask, properties and performers related, and composed a series of pictures illustrating for the audience the wider implications of what was often a fairly simple story.

The tragedians regularly introduced gods as characters. Often the sentiments and behaviour of these characters were ambivalent, even perverse, though no more so than the actions of the gods and goddesses of the Homeric poems. But each tragedian had his own way of relating human experience to the divine, not only by what these gods or demi-gods said, but how they were presented for the audience to see. The link between the putting-on of plays and the arts of sculpture and painting gained an extra dimension when the human actor took on divine attributes. The god became, in physical form, the personification of more abstract ideas and emotions. Accordingly he was presented as above human behaviour. This in itself became a stage image by placing the god literally above the humans, either on the roof of the setting, or 'flown' in on the crane. When a god appears at ground level it is always for a specific purpose. From this most basic of examples it is possible to see how the Greeks 'made' plays in full accordance with the physical and spatial properties of theatre as they have been understood ever since.

This is an age of image. Not only has television by its very nature turned us steadily into a generation of viewers, but the advertising agent has ensured that we daily face a barrage of colours and shapes guaranteed to make us salivate as inexorably as Pavlov's dogs at the sound of bells. In every walk of life we are invited to make associations, both consciously and unconsciously, and to create links between our sensory responses. This might seem to be, as Marshall McLuhan proposed, a phenomenon of the last hundred years, a consequence of living in an increasingly complex world. But it is not a wholly new phenomenon. In the comparatively simple world of classical Athens, most physical objects had a symbolic value. Gods and goddesses had aspects and areas of responsibility. The process of attribution grew from the need to make sense of a world which was not consistently rational. There was even a god of the irrational, appropriately Dionysus, also god of the theatre.

If the McLuhan analysis of the twentieth century seems now to be more a symptom of the 1960s than an evaluation for all time, there is no gainsaying the truism that the invention of the printing press seriously dislocated the way man looked at his world, and the invention of first the photograph, then the moving picture, were every bit as drastic in their implications. The widening from a purely European focus among artists and scholars in the present century coincided with, and largely contributed to, a view of other cultures and other periods through an indigenous term of reference rather than one imposed from outside. For better or worse this led to new forms of criticism. More productively it extended boundaries. It extended them but it did not abandon them, and though our experience of the image may have changed in time, the way in which the theatre promotes image would appear to have altered surprisingly little.

The form, style and presentation of Greek tragedies were, I believe, dictated by an understanding of image which permeated the whole of classical Athens, its education, its culture and its theology. Pandora's box, the Trojan horse, the stone of Sisyphus all represented a way of thinking. The theatre of the Athenians was a specific art form which transformed that way of thinking into living metaphors. There is no good reason to believe that, were we able to witness the first production of the *Oresteia* in 458 BC, we should find it more difficult to appreciate in its own terms than a black figure vase, or a *Noh* play which has its specialized conventions within a recognizable performance aesthetic.

The Athenian of the fifth century BC inhabited a city so beautiful, so cultivated and so proud of its achievements that anywhere else had to seem inferior. Athenians were citizens, the rest of the world barbarians. Sophocles and Euripides grew up in a community made confident by the defeat of the Persians, the rebuilding of the city and a naval and commercial supremacy. It was a confidence created by Aeschylus' generation, made manifest in a new political system which gave every male citizen a say in how his city should be governed. It is fashionable at present to decry the institutions and achievements of the Athenian democratic system for its dependence on slavery of one sort or another, but the attitudes of the time, at least when compared with those displayed elsewhere, were enlightened, or perhaps obfuscated, by ideals rather than dogma. They were based on a moral system which sprung partly from a polytheistic hierarchy and partly from convenient custom which was under constant revision, in detail if not substance. Lacking the authority of a fixed creed, the Athenians looked to their intellectuals for guidance as much as they did to their politicians and their holy men. The dramatists were by common agreement teachers who gave guidance about current issues in their tragedies, even though they were almost all located within the mythical framework of the Homeric world.

The civilization of classical Athens cannot really be accounted for. At a time when much of the rest of western Europe survived for the most part at a level of tribal feudalism, Athenian poets and philosophers were addressing themselves to questions of considerable sophistication on every topic under the sun. And if it was the Ionians who had speculated first about whether that sun might be a large, hot stone, rather than the god Apollo, it was the playwrights of Athens who considered, through the stage character of that same Apollo, the major paradoxes inherent in a religion which featured a set of gods whose moral sense was at odds with their supernatural powers. If the playwrights were well aware of a historical sense of progress, they knew too that this progress could best be evaluated by reason. It was reason which set Greek apart from outsider. It was reason upon which the Delphic precepts about self-knowledge and the dangers of excess were founded. It was the disavowal of reason which caused most anxiety to Euripides writing his *Andromache*, *Trojan Women* and *Bacchae*, when in Athens both politics and the conduct of war had become dominated by expediency and private interest.

The theatre was no isolated phenomenon. It developed and prospered at a time of renewal and progress. The drama epitomized both. It combined the sense of reason with artistic sensibility; it paraded mankind and his achievements while warning of the implications of placing too great a value upon those achievements; in linking mortal to immortal it synthesized the arts.

With the Persians defeated at Salamis in 480 BC, the sea-battle in which Aeschylus fought and the aftermath of which was the subject of his first extant play, the Athenians returned in triumph to a ruined city. They spent the next sixty years and a great deal of other people's money making the new Athens one of the most beautiful cities the world has seen. The Acropolis sprouted monuments, sanctuaries and temples, exquisite in form, with pediments topping the Doric and Ionic columns. Greatest of all was the Parthenon with its remarkable optical symmetry. Man might have been the measure of all things in Periclean Athens, but the architecture was god-size.

Nor were size and form exclusively Athenian. In architecture there was a common style throughout the Greek world. If private dwellings were usually small, a significantly high proportion of Greeks saw a temple or sanctuary every day of their lives. It is difficult not to believe that the impression would have been similar to that made in the fourteenth century on those who lived in the lee of such cathedrals as Beverley, York or Lincoln.

Of course it is no accident that Athenian art developed as its architecture and political system developed. They were fundamentally linked. The theatre of medieval England is commonly understood in the light of the visual arts of the time. In the same way we would be right to consider the presentation of plays in Athens as one aspect, or at least an extension of, classical art and architecture. We must consider too the effect on the art of the actor and the light cast on the theatrical sensibilities of playwrights and audiences. Art was a skill, as necessary to the whole life of the community as were the skills of seamanship, metal-work or masonry. The various crafts had their gods as patrons and protectors, as did the city itself crowned by the Parthenon with its massive statue of Athene. The playwrights and actors had their Dionysus.

Literature developed alongside sculpture and painting, but it was less available, even to those who could read. Hence the absence of 'criticism'. The Athenians could be critical but they were not critics. It is a mark of their personality as much as of their political system that the prizes in the dramatic competitions should have been awarded in accordance with a process which, if not arbitrary, at least ensured that no single person could be held responsible. The judges, one selected from each of the ten tribes, cast votes from which a random and anonymous five were decisive.

The system was not as haphazard as it would be today, if only because the criteria were based on common experience. Most Athenians saw the same plays on the same day and under the same conditions. From myth they were familiar with the themes and concepts which pervade the plays: light and dark, real life and dream, truth and falsehood, right and wrong, sight and blindness, life and death, god and man. Their ears were attuned to the argument and counter-argument of the Assembly, which all male citizens could attend, and their vision was dominated by the daily sights of the city. Corporately or individually the audience which Aeschylus, Sophocles and Euripides were writing to satisfy encompassed every aspect of Athenian life.

The Athenians chose to put on plays at festivals in winter and early spring, before the weather in Athens becomes hot. The audience attending the Theatre of Dionysus was large. For the most part they comprised male citizens on holiday, though there may have been some women present, wives, or more probably courtesans, the *hetaira* class who were not allowed to marry citizens. Children and resident aliens may also have attended, while foreign traders and ambassadors could be guests at the Great Dionysia. Most of them, at least in the latter half of the fifth century, paid for admission and had seats allocated by ticket. Organization and control were probably on a commercial basis, though many of the management details are unclear. Production costs came from government subsidy and private patronage.

Plays, it would seem, were received with attention and if the award of prizes was in the gift of the jury of ordinary spectators, no doubt the majority found ways of indicating to the judges their own enthusiasms and prejudices. Plato tells of numbers as high as 30,000 crowding into the Theatre of Dionysus, but a more conservative estimate suggests that 15,000 or 17,000 is the most that could be accommodated at any performance.

The spectators sat in the open air and at a distance from the actors. Those in the lower rows of seats were relatively close to the chorus. 'Relatively' could mean as close as a few feet to one or two individuals, though this afforded less chance to view the whole chorus in pattern. Important guests and the judges did sit this close, we are led to believe, but it may well be that these were not the 'best' seats for a total view of the play. From most of the seats in the steeply raked auditorium the chorus were seen against the floor, with the actors beyond them. If your seat was in the centre of the *theatron* and half-way back, you were perhaps 140 feet from the actors. From the back the distance was well over 200 feet. Clearly the playwrights were fully aware of this. Acting and staging were dominated by it. Though there were small local theatres in Attica and elsewhere, the Theatre of Dionysus in Athens set the standard, at least until well into the fourth century BC.

These are the incidentals of the tragic performance. They affected the way in which plays were received, but to bridge the gap between an Athenian perception and a modern response we must now consider *how* the Greeks saw and accordingly *what* they saw.

The best reason for being suspicious of antiquarian

reconstruction of the performances of the past is that, even were we able to reproduce with exactness the text, setting, costume and acting style of any former time, what we could never reproduce is the audience. The audience in Athens made a contribution to performance through a theatrical sophistication born of regular experience, which inspired Aeschylus, Sophocles and Euripides to constant experiment with their medium. In later chapters I hope to show how the form of presentation and the style of acting combined to make available to the playwrights a whole armoury of visual signs and devices to amplify and often to take over from the spoken word. But such a thing would only have been possible among a people whose perception was dictated as much by the eye as the ear.

The popularity of the theatre in Athens and its accessibility to such a large proportion of the population together offer some guarantee that we may consider the surviving plays as part of an immediate rather than an intellectual experience. The problems tragedy presents to a twentieth-century audience are formidable but there is a key to solving them. The *Oresteia*, in the form in which we now have it, is a complex poem commanding academic analysis for its structure, metre, language, imagery, philosophy, theology and political stance. That all or most of these complexities were apparent to the 15,000 traders, shopkeepers and craftsmen who crowded together to listen to the four or five hours of ode, dialogue and set speech, is difficult to credit. The *Oresteia* is also a great play. The traders and shopkeepers went not only to listen to it. They went to watch it, to witness a story unfold, a story which related to the history of their people and to their present concerns, a story which could affect them and move them, from which they could return to their homes uplifted, perhaps even purged.

It would do little service to the theatre to suggest that theatrical values exist only to make contact with those whom Aristotle chooses to identify as 'common persons'. There must have been, however, a level of immediate experience in Greek tragedy, and we need to decipher it if we are to discover the theatre's original appeal rather than help foster its esoteric reputation. What the audience saw in the Theatre of Dionysus was a means of story-telling with different layers and dimensions, only some of which would have been comprehended by any single individual.

None of this is to deny the narrative level, which was usually simple, or the ability of even the less educated to follow quite complex argument. In a society for which political influence meant skill at rhetoric in the Assembly, dialogue and set speech were familiar enough. Athenians were used to listening and to making decisions based on what they heard. They were familiar with spoken verse from the lyric poets who extolled famous men and their exploits and, more especially, from the epic poems, created in a time of oral tradition, which were still recited at the festivals when a formal text had been fixed. An audience familiar with listening to poetry may well have been able to follow the structure and language of an Aeschylean chorus.

That is the lyrical side of drama, the side which relates most closely to the text on the page. But the text, and by extension the voice of the actor which transmits the word to the audience, is never the whole performance in a theatre. The radio actor James Dale once compared acting for radio to cutting with half a pair of scissors. Though the actor's voice was an important part of his equipment in the classical theatre, it was only a part. Aeschylus and his successors were not cutting with half a pair of scissors. They had available all the equipment of an intensely physical form of presentation.

The more important layer of performance, and the one which has been most neglected in criticism, relates less to the actor's performance than to the playwright's exploitation of audience expectation within individual scenes or entire plays. In the second half of this book I hope to demonstrate how each of the tragedians explored the possibilities of the visual through stage picture, tableau and pattern to enhance prime themes and issues within a play. It is not nearly so obvious on the page how a major dramatist may explore the most basic of stage devices. How easy it is to forget, in the study, the contribution of a third actor to a scene where the lines are divided between the other two, or to overlook the significance of a scenic unit or stage property, or the performers' physical relationship to it. By considering all the extant plays, however briefly, I believe it is possible to show that the Athenian tragedians not only wrote with an audience in mind, but consciously used the stage image to condense an issue or a conflict in vivid microcosm.

The writing and producing of tragedy was initially, if never quite exclusively, an Athenian province. Drama is a medium which arises from, and is a reflection of, the temper of the times. Plays are about people and passions and ideas. Ancient Greek tragedy is very Greek. More specifically it is very Athenian. If this seems to set up a barrier which it is difficult for the modern reader or playgoer to overcome, there is the consolation that the emotions which are the substance of tragedy are as poignant and accessible as ever they were. It is only the 'Greekness' of Greek tragedy with which one needs to come to terms, not its 'ancientness'. The theatricality may not always be obvious on the page. It may have become submerged by the linguistic and literary detail which has tended to dominate classical scholarship. But there can no longer be any doubt that in the plays which survived we have scripts for performers, geared to all the resources of an elaborate theatre and a responsive and alert audience.

It is necessary to look first at those physical aspects of the Greek stage which the playwrights could rely upon, aspects sufficiently familiar to the audiences for them to become useful to a dramatist in search of new ways to tell his story. Here the theatre is not an isolated form but a part of a complex culture. How the Greeks understood their theatre is related to how they regarded the architecture of their city, the shapes they saw around them every day, indeed all those functional and decorative objects which created the pattern of day-to-day living as well as of special occasions.

3

THE STAGE

In *The Waning of the Middle Ages* Johan Huizinga wrote that 'In an epoch of pre-eminently visual inspiration, like the fifteenth century, pictorial expression easily surpasses literary expression. Although representing only the visual forms of things, painting nevertheless expresses a powerful inner sense, which literature when it limits itself to describing externals wholly fails to do'.[1] Pindar and Thucydides notwithstanding, much the same could be said of the Athens of Pericles, and if not Athens, the rest of Greece in the fifth and fourth centuries BC. Though forms of government were so diverse that periods of peace were exceptional, there was a universality of reference in religious and artistic expression which the tragic theatre of Athens both typified and exploited. This being so, the difficulty of deciphering the details of the original staging of the tragedies becomes less of a problem.

The religious aspect of public festival is now less prominent in the west than it is in the east, where it is still possible to witness, if not to participate in, a celebration of the life of the spirit. The first experience of even a package-tour trance-dance can be sufficiently disturbing to suggest to the open-minded

1 *The Waning of the Middle Ages*, trans. F. Hopman, Harmondsworth, Penguin, 1955, p. 295.

that Hamlet's injunction to Horatio about the things in heaven and earth has not quite lost its force in our shrinking world. Nor is there anything revolutionary in suggesting that a search for the Greek sense of theatre may well find more points of contact in an oriental rather than an occidental tradition.

There are two principal reasons for this. Firstly, all forms of theatre and dance in India and Indonesia, China and Japan, whether 'high' or 'low' art, have resisted the move towards realism. Various art forms are closely woven into cultural and religious patterns which change little. Such continuity has ensured a continuity of artistic practice. Training for the performing arts is exceedingly long in the east and is based more on imitation than self-expression. As a result the world of the stage has remained a world of artifice.

Secondly, though less claim can be made for this as an oriental manifestation, the theatre forms of the east have never ceased to integrate a variety of visual and plastic modes which wholly reflect the expression of their peoples. The same claim cannot really be made for Europe beyond the Renaissance, but in the Athens of the fifth century BC there blossomed a rare civilization which both matched and was exemplified by its cultural achievement.

Theatrical technique during the seventy years between the first and last surviving tragedies was not static. Any study of the fifth-century tragedians is notable more for the differences it reveals between Aeschylus, Sophocles and Euripides than for their similarities. The theatre of the Athenians was narrow in neither reference nor influence. It reflected its time and the temperament of its people, as the theatre always has. It also encapsulated a way of looking at life, a way of seeing the surrounding world.

In such a culture the force of allegory is strong. Even stronger, I have suggested, was the power of image in the Athenian theatre. The audiences were used to seeing painting and sculpture in which the dramatic scene was condensed, again as in medieval art. Euripides' *Children of Heracles* opens with the old man Iolaus seeking sanctuary with the sons of Heracles at the temple of Zeus at Marathon, threatened by Copreus, the herald of Eurystheus, who wants to take them back to Argos. In 1963 a red figure vase, dated at about 400 BC, was discovered which appears to offer a composite view of the opening scene (figure 1). On it we see an old man standing on a plinth beside a single Ionic column which is topped by a statue of Zeus. Iolaus, if it is he, carries a suppliant branch of olive and a traveller's staff. There are four children wearing olive wreaths, two of them carrying branches as well, the other two clinging to the old man. A fifth boy is featured at the top of the vase – in the play Hyllus has gone with the older boys to look for an alternative refuge. Approaching at one side is a herald with herald's wand and traveller's staff. This would be Copreus coming from abroad, wearing actor's knee-length boots. To the other side stands Athene, Athens itself, with helmet, staff and shield.

Every element of the scene is included on the vase down to the attitude of the characters: the fearful children clasping the old man's robe; Iolaus himself with legs awkwardly crossed as he leans in towards the column; Copreus threatening, arrogant, hand on hip; Athene on the front foot, but protective. The cult statue of Zeus indicates that the scene is Marathon. Each aspect is represented and identified emblematically, giving not a production 'still', but a composite scene. Characters are identified by property, location by column and statue, theatricality by stage costume and attitude.

There are plenty of similar examples, whose implications for stage performance are of major significance. Two columns and a pediment seem to indicate that a scene had been inspired by a stage performance. Some scenes show double doors in the *paraskenia* or side-wings (figures 2 and 3). Others show stage furniture and properties – tombs, beds, urns, swords and axes. On these and other vases we are given an impression inspired by a drama, and it is not unreasonable to make at least some proposition from them about the physical appearance of the theatre and its settings.

Many of these vases, however, date from the fourth century BC and are not from Athens anyway. At first sight this would seem to diminish their value in the present context, but the effect may prove to be the opposite if they represent for the Greek world just that universality that Huizinga implies for the medieval. Apart from the 'theatrical vases' there are three ways in which we can approach the question of stage settings. We can theorize on what the theatre 'ought' to have looked like in order to fit in with its surroundings; we can make an educated guess at what it looked like by the time that Aristotle was writing and

Figure 1 Children of Heracles, Policoro vase, *c.*400 BC (Museo Nazionale della Siritide, Policoro)

Figure 2   Eumenides, Gnathia vase, *c.*350 BC (Hermitage Museum, Leningrad)

Figure 3   *Iphigeneia in Tauris*, Campanian vase, *c*.330 BC (Musée du Louvre)

work backwards; and we can examine the surviving plays to see what they seem to prescribe. We could also look much further forward to the writers of the Roman empire, to Vitruvius and Pollux, were it not that their pronouncements are so contrary and confused as to be virtually no help to the present study. In isolation none of these approaches is too promising; together they can be found, if not to provide direct answers, at least to establish some useful general principles.

The fifth-century Athenians inhabited a world of superb artistic form. Wherever they went in their daily work the contours and dimensions of stoa or statuary were so much a part of their consciousness as to account for, and indeed justify, Pericles' own parade of the Athenian love of beauty, as recorded by Thucydides in the famous funeral oration. It was not only the shape of the public buildings which informed the consciousness of the Athenian people, but their decoration too. Though the paint has peeled off with the years, every indication is that the city presented not a desert of white marble, but a pageant of blues, reds, golds and silvers every bit as vivid as those supplied by Sir Arthur Evans in his restoration of Knossos. Public buildings were attractive to the eye, temples and statues were of massive size and elaborate ornamentation befitting the gods in whose honour they had been set up.

The theatre was surely no exception. The *skene* which backed the actors may not have offered a realistic reconstruction of the area it represented, but it is likely to have presented to the audience an aspect which was both artistically pleasing and familiar. The appearance of the actor and the nature of his performance stem from this general aesthetic and the playwrights made use, as have playwrights since, of the audience's understanding of certain artistic principles.

It is usually accepted that the playing-place in Athens went through five major stages of development. If, for the sake of argument, tragedy was first performed at the Great Dionysia about the year 532 BC, then for the next thirty years or so it was probably staged in makeshift conditions in the *Agora*. About the year 500 BC, perhaps because of a collapse of seating, the playing-place was moved to its present site, south-east of the Acropolis. The traces of that theatre, for which Aeschylus constructed all his mature plays and for which Sophocles began to write, are so meagre that archaeologists now dispute whether the few stones which do remain even indicate a circular *orchestra* as a feature of the theatre of the first half of the fifth century. But this was the home of the Great Dionysia until Pericles initiated, soon after the middle of the century, the building programme which took most of the rest of it to complete. A major part of that programme involved the transformation of the Precinct of Dionysus which included the playing-place usually known as the Periclean theatre.

The Periclean theatre represents the third home of drama in Athens. The material features are simple enough. The *orchestra* was circular, flanked on just over half its circumference by an auditorium. A stage building, or *skene*, ran at a tangent to the further edge of the circle, or just beyond it, leaving room for the actors to perform between *skene* and *orchestra*. The Precinct contained other buildings, the *Odeion*, which was a roofed chamber in which certain preliminaries were conducted, a long hall behind the *skene* and a temple to one side of it.

The conversion from second theatre to third seems to have taken many years and, even when completed, the Periclean theatre was not thought of as permanent. The first 'permanent' theatre in Athens was constructed under the direction of Lycurgus around the year 330 BC. This was the fourth stage of development, the fifth being the 'romanization' which transformed the theatre into its present state, with low stone stage and semi-circular paved *orchestra*.

It was for the 'impermanent' Periclean theatre that all the surviving plays of Sophocles, Euripides and Aristophanes, thirty-seven in all, were written, and yet far more is known about the stone building which replaced it.

The difference between the permanent theatre and the non-permanent one was that in the permanent one the *skene* and the stage could not be moved. Made of brick or stone there they were built, and there they stayed, at least, in Athens, until the Romans intervened. In the Periclean theatre it was not so. That is the broad principle, though it is worth noting that neither form precludes 'scenery'.

The details present more of a problem. For two hundred years between the innovations of Thespis and the stone theatre built by Lycurgus, the feature of stage and setting was mobility. By implication that means versatility and there are clues as to what this versatility involved. By the end of the fourth century BC and the beginning of the third, permanent theatres were sprouting all over the Greek world. The Lycurgan *skene* in Athens eventually succumbed to Roman adaptation but the performance spaces of the late classical and Hellenistic theatres have enough in common to hint at the Athenian version.

The background consists of a single-storey stage building with a columned facade and topped by a tiled or sometimes a flat roof. The acting area is confined by *paraskenia*, side-wings, constructed as columned porches with a pedimental top and double doors to match the central entrance.

If the first 'permanent' theatre in Athens was built to super-sede an impermanent version, two important features of the first can be reasonably assumed. Firstly, all the major elements of the Periclean *skene* were removable in section or *in toto*. Secondly, the first permanent theatre was designed not as a revolutionary concept but as a solid composite version of the most convenient arrangement of the temporary theatre. By inference then, it is fairly safe to assume that in the Periclean theatre for which Sophocles and Euripides were writing, the playwrights had available to them a system of wooden, hence portable, pillars and a number of changeable units to define the space either vertically or horizontally, or both. These units formed the scenic background in combinations which could accommodate any Greek play we know about. They are not 'scenic decoration', the *skenographia*, which Aristotle tanta-lizingly attributed to Sophocles. But if Sophocles did introduce 'scenic decoration', and there is no reason to doubt Aristotle on this point, what precisely was it? And what was used instead, before Sophocles employed it?

It is at this point that the plays themselves come into the argument, though not as a last resort, and in the understanding that there is no absolute reason why any play ever written should not be performed in the middle of a car park.

The first positive note is struck by the fact that there is a clear difference between the way Aeschylus refers to the background in his early plays and in his last extant work, the *Oresteia*, composed well after Sophocles had begun to exhibit. The set-tings of the earlier pieces are identified in terms sufficiently vague for numbers of commentators, the most recent among them, to assume that there was no stage building at all. It has been inferred, for example, that because Queen Atossa in *Persians* asserts positively on her second entrance that she has *not* come in a chariot, that she *did* make her first entrance in a chariot. Further, if she arrives from her palace on either entrance, then the palace must be far enough away from the scene of the action to make it worth coming by chariot sometimes. The setting therefore cannot represent her palace, and accordingly there is no setting. The logic appears to be sound enough, or would be, but for the chorus having indicated a few lines before the Queen enters at all that they are sitting 'beside this ancient roof'. That, the argument goes, must be to indicate that the chorus are to be thought of as *inside* a council chamber. Here, of course, ordinary logic breaks down. If the chorus in the *orchestra* are inside a council chamber, how could Atossa think of driving her chariot into it anyway?

The answer, I would suggest, is not one of ordinary logic but of stage logic: stage logic that stems not from there being no stage background at all, but from the presence of a permanent *skene* which can be whatever Aeschylus requires it to be. It frames and backs a comprehensive series of pictures. Aeschylus crafted his plays in accordance with a sense of image far outside the logic of realism. It is not realistic that Electra in *Libation-Bearers* identifies her brother from his footprints on the stage floor or in the *orchestra*. It is theatrically right that she should copy his pose and thereby discover his presence. This is the Aeschylean theatre, mocked by the realist Euripides less than fifty years later, but not to be dismissed for that. Behind the Aeschylean use of setting there is a theatrical mind not confined by individual reference.

Such an argument might seem to open the door to absolutely any kind of interpretation of any aspect of the plays, were Aeschylus not bound by a sense of allegory so compellingly in tune with much of the theatre since his time. One can even propose a conscious relationship between the human figure and his background of a similar nature to that found in much of the art of the period. The human being is not isolated in space, in art or in drama. He is defined by relation to other human beings and against physical objects which enhance the statement or purpose of the words. This should affect our understanding both of the nature of Greek acting and of the manner in which Aeschylus built his plays. I hope to show later that in all his surviving work Aeschylus promoted a central dominant idea at a variety of levels.

Seven Against Thebes has its action somewhere inside the city-walls of Thebes, with enemy audibly threatening from outside. *Prometheus* takes place on a mountain in Scythia, *Suppliants* at a sacred precinct which can be used as sanctuary. None of these plays is unstageable without a central entrance. All of them would have been enhanced by presentation against a *skene*. If these three, together with *Persians*, were originally performed in front of a wooden facade, the *skene* had probably, by the time of Aeschylus, become in its own right an expression of stage place. The *skene* was not employed, I would suggest, only when it became necessary to indicate a habitable background. The play was a play by virtue of the action taking place in front of the *skene*.

The *Oresteia* does make use of the central entrance in all three parts, and in *Eumenides* has a change of location in mid-action from Delphi to Athens. The difference between the four earlier plays and the Oresteian trilogy is not a difference between four plays which did not need a *skene* and three which did, but between four plays which used the *skene* to define stage space and a connected trilogy in which the form of that *skene* is made to identify somewhere specific.

In the plays of Sophocles, Euripides and indeed Aristophanes, flexible use of location shows the possibilities for the stage by the end of the century. Settings vary from the single palace entrance, which suffices for a majority of tragedies, to the setting of *Ajax* which moves from tent to seashore, the decorated porticoes of Delphi to which the Chorus draw specific attention in Euripides' *Ion* and the fluid fantasy of Aristophanes' mid-air Cloudcuckooland in *Birds* or river Styx in *Frogs*. This flexibility certainly makes sense as part of a progression which begins with the *skene* of Aeschylus, a template for plays produced in the pre-Periclean theatre, and concludes with the fixing of the stone *skene* in the time of Lycurgus.

What accounts for the change between the non-specific *skene* of earlier Aeschylus and the more specific, though versatile, *skene* of the *Oresteia* may well have been Sophocles' introduction of 'scenic decoration', though the Roman architect Vitruvius credited the painter Agatharchus with employing the principles of perspective on behalf of Aeschylus. Agatharchus,

Vitruvius records, inspired Democritus and Anaxagoras in the use of perspective 'so that, by this deception, a fruitful representation of the appearance of buildings might be given in painted scenes'. This is tenuous evidence for a representational perspective facade as stage setting, if only because Vitruvius was not writing until the time of Augustus, but it does accord with a general stage principle applicable to all of the Greek tragedies.

It may be that Agatharchus' contribution was to give specific form to what had previously been an undecorated, and hence, neutral means of framing the stage action. Merely to show in two-dimensional painting, however clever the perspective effect, what had previously been visible architecturally in three dimensions, could only have been a retrogade step. So what Agatharchus contributed to stage design, or perhaps Sophocles if we prefer to trust Aristotle's account, was to paint a *part* of the setting in order to identify the *whole*.

In some later theatres the stone columns of the *skene* still contain the grooves which would have accommodated wooden panels. Known as *pinakes* in the Hellenistic theatre these panels seem to have been painted with scenic emblems. In Vitruvius' plans of a theatre of his own time he includes a refinement of the *pinakes*, prismatic pieces known as *periaktoi*, which could swivel to present any of three sides to the audience. The late grammarian Pollux was under the impression that even *periaktoi* were in use in the theatre of the classical period, and, though many of his assumptions appear wildly inaccurate and are supported by no independent evidence, he was not necessarily wrong about everything.

Whatever the details, we can work on the assumption that the setting for plays in the Periclean theatre, if not before, may have involved a familiar though flexible scenic facade with individual locations identified by some form of painted detail on panels placed between the columns on either side of the central double door. Porticoes, pediments and roof platforms all added variety to meet special needs and panels were either replaced between plays, or even swivelled if *periaktoi* were in use so early. Such a solution is hardly novel, but its plausibility in the present context makes a specific contribution because of the artistic principles governing the way in which the panels were decorated. Even from the restricted number of plays we have, it is quite possible to discern how, in the last years of his career, Aeschylus expanded the possibilities of the stage picture by juxtaposing the human figure with inanimate objects. Action was placed against a background. The actor was mobile, the background static. Moreover, the foreground was highly animated by the chorus. In broadest terms, the background needed to present information which would enhance the play. Here surely is the one area in which stage technique did develop from the time of Aeschylus to that of Euripides. The caves, seashores and peasant huts of Sophocles and Euripides became such not merely because the playwrights put into the mouths of their characters words which said so, but because the panels of the setting identified them as such. This is not realism, nor is it probable that the painting was intended to recreate the actual setting. Rather, it is in keeping with the principles of iconography found in Greek art of the time which identify place by cult statue and patron god or goddess by costume, by property, by hairstyle and by colour. Here is the all-important link between active drama and the vase-painting encapsulating the dramatic scene.

It may well be that no two plays ever had the same setting, even if they were both set 'in front of a palace'. The setting could have suggested the equivalent of a caption or perhaps some major theme of the play. That four plays were presented in harness, even when the connected tetralogy was no longer the fashion, suggests common themes within a group of plays, themes which might have been emphasized by the form of the decor from play to play.

The question remains as to how effective a panel of no more than thirty square feet would have been in so large a theatre. Distance would have denied all but the most basic of information to the higher rows of the Periclean auditorium, but if it was possible to pick out the human figure of the actor, it would have been possible to identify the representation of a god of human size or above, or of a grove, a palace, a deserted place or a cave. If the audience were used to 'reading' painting and sculpture, the formalized shorthand would already have been familiar and that much easier to recognize.

This is the common factor, I believe, which unites the staging practice of the plays we possess. The stage is defined, as on so many of the intriguing but elusive 'theatrical' vases, by its formal *skene*. Individual places are defined by the convention of the parallel arts of vase-painting and frieze. As the century proceeds stage display develops its third dimension as scenic units and devices blend more fully with the actor and the performance dimension of the chorus becomes less pronounced.

By the end of the fifth century BC, the *mechane*, or stage crane, and the *ekkuklema*, wheeled platform, were in use in old comedy. Aristophanes refers to them in his plays. By inference they were used in tragedy too, Aristophanes appearing to parody Euripides' use of them. Quaint though such devices might seem in the light of subsequent machine stages, their significance resides far less in the tenuous connection with a new realism than in the way in which they throw light on the working of theatrical imagination. The crane was a refinement of the simple and basic idea that a god appeared above mere mortals, sometimes visible to them, sometimes not. Even by the time of *Prometheus*, Aeschylus had seen the visual potential of juxtaposing earthly and heavenly character and argument by reference to the physical position of man and god. If such a belief goes beyond our understanding of how that particular play could be, never mind was, staged, the opening of the *Oresteia*, with a watchman on the palace roof, bears indisputable witness to the use of an upper level for the purpose of some kind of visual contrast. Sophocles used the device of the *deus ex machina* sparingly, though the Athene who appears in *Ajax* above the scene throws special emphasis onto mankind below. Euripides frequently framed his plays with a god or gods in order to contrast received myth with human behaviour. For Euripides a god was identified by virtue of being 'flown in', physically removed from the earth-bound world of human beings.

The staging device of the crane may well have been a Euripidean invention. Placed to the side and behind the *skene*, the *mechane* apparently hoisted the actor over the top of the playing-space. If Helen arrived with Apollo in one play and Castor with Pollux in another, it must have consisted of more than a simple harness, while the anxious 'aside' of Trygaeus to the *mechanopoios*, the crane-operator, in Aristophanes' *Peace*, suggests it was every bit as precarious as it sounds. It is even tempting to wonder if Euripides was aware of the spurious dignity the crane imposed, and consciously employed it to comment on the relationship of god and man as he portrayed it in his plays, a relationship often creaking at the hinges and faintly ridiculous.

The *ekkuklema* involved a similar principle. Functioning in all probability as a simple platform wheeled out from inside the *skene*, the *ekkuklema* was a practical demonstration of the tableau. Stage furnishings, dead bodies, or, in an extreme Aristophanic example, the playwright Euripides at work in his study, could be presented with the maximum of convenience and withdrawn with the minimum of fuss. Here again we do not have simply a solution to a problem, that of how to present what would logically stay indoors. Instead we find the basic stage principle of the 'reveal', the sudden display of a prepared visual sequence to give enhanced significance. This is no stagey device of temporary appeal. It is part of the stock-in-trade of playwrights through the ages. The reveal gave birth to the trap, to the front curtain and even to the blackout. Its use by Aeschylus in the *Oresteia*, and perhaps earlier, is with a full understanding of the effect of the device, whether it showed parallel tableaux of slaughtered bodies or the Furies themselves snoozing noisily.

The two areas marked out by the *mechane* and the *ekkuklema*, that is above the stage and behind it, increase the scope of the theatre. To the Greek audience, the stage still remained the stage, a place of art and artifice where the imagination did not make do for reality but tempered it, giving objects significance and the stage picture a level of metaphor. The result was that each tragedian felt free to explore the nature of place as well as time in a novel way, nothing to do with any laws of Unity.

The reason for laying such stress on the conscious command of the stage by the Greek playwrights is that it is only too easy to become bogged down in unanswerable questions about the original staging in the Greek theatre, rather than address oneself to matters of stage space and time which are accessible. It is possible to read the extant plays with a practitioner's eye and take from the page a vision which is at least enhanced by, perhaps even dependent upon, the physical conditions of the stage. The variety of places that the background might be called upon to define fits perfectly with a refined tradition of theatrical emblem which extended to costume and property and ultimately to the performance of actor and chorus.

4
THE PERFORMERS

There is a telling remark in J.J. Pollitt's *Art and Experience in Classical Greece* when the author tells us that 'Early Classical statues tend to be dramatic, and to carry with them the impression that they represent one distinct stage in a series of events'.[1] This is helpful in the present study because it allows us to consider Greek acting as well not in isolation but in relation to other art forms. The art of acting was developing in Athens alongside changes in the styles of painting and sculpture. The dynamic of a carved figure may well, as Pollitt implies, reflect a frozen moment in a mobile pageant. The fact that a moment in a play might be frozen in a similar way could indicate that the earliest acting was of a stylized nature which crystallized emotions and tensions and held them static. The most graphic theatre portraits tend to be those from periods of heightened acting. Kean's Othello or Garrick's Lear were praised by contemporary critics for the vibrancy of the personality behind them and the quality of the actors' diction, but their essence can at least be glimpsed from engravings. The graphic mode of melodrama is more easily conjured from photograph than is the Shavian comedy.

The nearest anyone today can come to the action and performance of a play from the Athens of Aeschylus is not through the

1 *Art and Experience in Classical Greece*, Cambridge, Cambridge University Press, 1952, p. 15.

words which have survived in formal text but through the postures of Athenian art, even when the figures adorn scenes which
have no direct connection with any known dramatic sequence.
Pollitt would go further: 'Sculptors and painters seem, in fact,
actually to have borrowed some of the technical devices which
had been developed in dramatic performances to convey character and narrative action – for example the formal gestures of
actors, the masks which were designed to express at once an
individual character and a basic type, and perhaps also a
dramatic sense of timing'.[2]

This is a refreshing claim which helps free the drama from its
isolation as an art form. It is also a slightly damaging one for the
ease with which it permits the unobservant to relegate the real
nature of the Greek theatre to that of the fossil.

Karl Mantzius was one of a rare breed to have combined
scholarship with theatrical expertise. Actor and director at the
Royal Theatre in Copenhagen, he was awarded a doctorate at
the University of Copenhagen in 1901 by defending his thesis
on the history of the English theatre. He was soon to publish a
six-volume history of the theatre, the first volume of which
dealt with the theatre of China, Japan, India, Greece and Rome.
An a-chronological approach was justified for the similarities
he saw between a variety of theatrical traditions which had in
common origins in religious practice and dramatic dance.

Mantzius devoted a whole chapter of the section on Greek
theatre to actors. Despite a number of assertions which hardly
stand up in the light of more formal and indeed more modern
scholarship, he takes considerable credit for being among the
first to consider Greek drama as a performance art. His understanding of the actor in classical Athens is summed up as follows: 'That these strangely equipped large figures with their
immovable faces which seemed petrified with suffering, and in
their gorgeous splendour, advancing slowly with solemn measured movements, must have produced a powerful and romantic
impression on the minds of the naïve ancient Greeks, we can
easily imagine. They must have appeared almost like living
images of the gods, and when the people heard the beautiful
grave words emanating from these walking statues, they were

2 ibid., p. 27.

seized with artistic as well as religious enthusiasm'.[3]

In these two sentences Mantzius manages to undermine almost everything of value he has said elsewhere. Allowing that any assessment of the Greeks as 'naïve' was more the mark of a patronizing generation than a studied analysis of the Greek temper, it is at best disappointing, if not a matter for dismay, that any practising actor, even at the turn of this century, should have so poor an understanding of the mask as a theatre weapon.

Mantzius' view of the actor in Athens was dictated by the belief of his time that in the fifth century BC he wore high boots and an exaggerated mask, and that he looked and performed as did his counterpart in the Rome of seven hundred years later. The Roman writer Lucian then complained of the grotesque mask and padded features of the actor of his day. That the actor of Lucian's time bore little resemblance to the actor in classical Athens is now generally accepted, but the confusion of the two was widespread for many years and led directly to an over-emphasis on the spoken word as the actor's main means of communication in both Athenian and Roman theatre, an over-emphasis which has not yet outgrown the premise on which it was based. This in its turn has prevented any adequate study of the differences between what Aeschylus and Euripides, writing in the same century, expected of their performers, even though their writing must have been influenced to a major extent by the possibilities of a practical rather than a theoretical art.

I have already suggested that the performance of the actor and, to some extent, the chorus, existed by reference to painting, to sculpture and to a sense of line and shape which provided a common aesthetic of the human form in space. The starting point for identifying what was unique in the performance in Athens was the mask (figure 4).

When an actor puts on a mask, he immediately suffers severe loss of vision. This is not so severe as to be incapacitating but is still sufficient to cause a certain amount of disorientation in the actor experiencing it for the first time. The main focus is not changed but the peripheral vision is cut to a dark edge. Most of what is sensed, rather than seen in the corner of the eye, ceases

3 *A History of Theatrical Art*, vol. 1, trans. L. von Cossel, London, Duckworth, 1903, p. 187.

Figure 4 Tragic mask and platform stage, Lucanian vase, *c*.330 BC (British Museum)

to exist. The effect is not unlike looking through a letter-box
compared with looking through a window.

The first reaction is to try to reorganize the balance of the
senses. The person with normal vision attunes it to his other
senses automatically and corrects the balance according to circumstance. The wearing of a mask reorders the senses and
alters the means of conveying and receiving information. Loss
of peripheral vision requires the wearer to move the whole head
instead of the pupil alone in order to look right or left, up or
down. In a theatre as large as the Theatre of Dionysus, the
unmasked actor might be able to see the whole audience. This
the masked actor could not do. In compensation, the masked
actor discovers that it is possible to relate the position of the
head to the rest of the body, so that the whole head is given
outline and meaning by the way in which it relates to neck,
shoulder, torso and stance. The human figure becomes more
indeed like a piece of sculpture, in which each line and curve
complements the dominant emotion. The difference from a
piece of sculpture is that the outline is fluid. The frozen position is as valuable to the actor as the held note in music. It is no
strain on the analogy to say that the masked actor and the
masked dancer 'compose' their performances.

Perhaps it could be argued that this is what any good actor
does who is not wearing a mask, but one needs only to witness a
performance by actors in masks who have not made physical
presentation their priority to realize how pointless the mask is
without a style of acting appropriate to it. As Keith Johnstone
records, 'You can watch a marvellous actor from the back of a
big theatre, his face just a microdot on the retina, and have the
illusion you've seen every tiny expression. Such an actor can
make a wooden mask smile, its carved lips tremble, its painted
brows narrow'.[4] When the masked actor reorders his senses he
removes some of the emphasis from his face, but also draws
attention to it. This does not diminish subtlety. It means that
he gives greater emphasis to other aspects of his physique as
they relate to the mask, so that each or any part of the body may
become as graphic as any other. The elated Hamlet may have
elated feet, elated hands, elated shoulders, but the audience is
drawn to the face to see just how elated he really is. The stubborn

4 *Impro*, London, Methuen, 1981, p. 185.

Antigone not only needs to be stubborn in each aspect of her being, but in such a way as to draw attention to the face through the whole person.

Much of what I have said above will seem so obvious to any dancer that it hardly needs stating at all. Why it is so important is that the performances of actor and dancer come together with the mask. It has now penetrated the comprehension of even those most wedded to the text that a Greek chorus were dancers first, because that is what the word means, and singers second. It is still all too common to find that no relation is made between the nature of the chorus in performance and the nature of the actor in Greek tragedy.

Once the actor has become familiar with wearing a mask, and has begun to explore the possibilities of a more graphic style of acting, he may become used quite quickly to the idea of acting as a 'demonstration'. The first real breakthrough comes at the point at which he no longer uses his facial muscles inside the mask. He discovers that a character can smile without his smiling. He does not need to weep inside the mask in order to make the mask weep. He comes to understand from the inside how it is that the mask is not bound or limited in the range of emotions it may express.

It requires no wide reading of Greek tragedy to realize that the characters in the plays of all three tragedians have a contrasting range of emotions to display. The reciter of the epic poems was assessed no less than the orator by his ability to amplify his argument by tone and gesture. For the actor in a mask these are not enough. Gesture might perhaps be defined as the under-lining of a point in argument by means of a physical counterpart to the voice. Real physical acting is more than this. The masked actor, as Gordon Craig, a contemporary of Mantzius, was the first to spell out in modern times, was more dancer than orator. The orator appears to his audience to be shocked, angered or dismayed. So does the modern actor who is unmasked. The masked actor has a new language at his disposal, or rather, the oldest acting language of all. Released from any requirement to copy the emotions he sees and uses in everyday life, his task is to translate these emotions into the language of the theatre, without diminishing them and their effect on an audience. Max Frisch, the Swiss playwright and novelist, wrote in his diary of the virtue of the puppet as being the best means to give life to an

Athene or a Zeus. Craig found inspiration in the Greek theatre in his search for the *über-marionette*, less a puppet than an inspired actor divorced from the 'mortality' of the actors of his day. The Athenian playwrights had that actor available to them. They never apologized for his shortcomings, or felt restricted by his limitations. They appreciated that in the mask they had the very basis and cornerstone of the new art that they and they alone in the ancient world had cultivated.

The thoughtful actor, even the one trained to look for motive first and to hope that the rest will follow, can usually come to appreciate this rather sooner than the literary critic. This is why it is all the more regrettable that Mantzius could talk about Greek actors as though they were some form of Victorian automata rather than the means whereby the rawest emotion was transmitted to a huge group of spectators.

To start with the mask is not to confine Greek acting to it. It was a part of the actor's externals, as were any other aspects of his costume, though there is evidence that he regarded it as central to his performance. But the actor himself was only a part of the stage composite which related him to both background and foreground and attuned his physical aspect to the words he spoke and the situation in which his character was placed.

Because only the written part of the plays has survived, Greek tragedy can often seem a harsh and forbidding genre. In attempting to restore some of the life by concentrating on the theatrical qualities, I would not wish to underestimate the aural side of the presentation. There is no lack of anecdote, apocryphal though some of it may be, to indicate that the audience did listen as well as watch and that the actor trained his voice to cope with the demands of a large open-air theatre. The actor who failed to meet the audience's demanding standards could expect little sympathy. The acoustic qualities of theatres such as the one at Epidaurus are well attested, though listening to the drop of a coin or the recitation of a brief passage is noticeably different from attending to the performance of a whole group of plays. Professor Benjamin Hunningher, who declared himself dubious about the ability of any actor to be audible throughout the *theatron* in Athens, had perhaps never had the benefit of witnessing a modern performance in an ancient theatre.⁵ The acoustics of a theatre are very different when the auditorium is full from when it is empty, and the effects of mask, costume and scenic background cannot be ignored even if they cannot be gauged with any accuracy. Nor have we any knowledge of how the voice was used, in particular in relation to the music which is likely to have accompanied it. Hunningher did have a point, though, when he suggested that the nature of dramatic performance was perhaps 'much closer to ballet opera than to the legitimate theatre'.⁶ Without quibbling too much over the precise definition of Hunningher's terms, it is undeniable that the Greek actor did perform in the context of both music and dance. The spoken word was so far from being the only means of expression as to have been unlikely to convey much meaning to the spectators without the more physical aspects of the whole theatre.

The surviving plays are written in a variety of metres from the basic iambic of dialogue and set speech to trochee and dochmiac, which reflect the differences in language of the formal and choral exchanges. Exactly how this variation related to either the vocal delivery of chorus or actor, or to the music, is an area of speculation completely beyond verification. It may be that a lyric rhythm in the script is an indication that some passage was originally intoned or sung. It seems unlikely that there was any use of what we could describe as harmony in the choral delivery, but it is not impossible that at times the human voice was in harmony with, or counterpointed by, the musical accompaniment. Pipe music was usually classified by mode, a variety of modes being possible, perhaps corresponding to mood. These are likely to have changed no less than other aspects of Athenian art as the century progressed and the language of the plays changed from the more solemn rhythms of Aeschylus to the fluid choruses and fluent dialogue of Euripides. A parallel between music and metre is attested not only by the comparative reliability of using metrical structure to date plays, but also by the word *rhuthmos* which can be used to define both sound and motion. For Plato, writing at the beginning of the fourth century BC, *rhuthmos* implies order and

5 *Acoustics and Acting in the Theatre of Dionysus Eleuthereus*, Amsterdam, N.V. Noord-Hollandsche Uitgevers Maatschappiz, 1956, pp. 7–13.
6 ibid., p. 23.

harmony, while within Euripides' plays it has the sense of 'a correct arrangement of elements' or 'the right way of doing things', much as the English 'rhythm' implies in the phrase 'the rhythm of life'. A sense of proportion is a dominating feature of Greek artistic momentum during the fifth century and it is frustrating to have so little direct sense of how it was expressed in Greek music. All that can be said with any confidence is that the Greek actor and chorus 'used' music, the playwright wrote with music in mind as a performance element and that vocal delivery was heightened in some parts of the play in accordance with the music that was being played. That the Greek actor ever sounded as unearthly as the actor of the Japanese *Kabuki*, with his strangulated delivery dredged up from deep inside his being, is unlikely if only because of the number of lines he had to get through and the complexity of their sentiments, but the relationship between musician and actor found in the *Noh* or in Pekin Opera might offer a serious parallel.

The complete loss of Greek music would be more of a handicap to understanding the essence of Greek theatre were it not for our growing understanding of the possibilities of dance. Dancing was a normal part of Greek expression, not only within Athenian culture but throughout the Greek world. Indeed in almost every culture known to anthropologists, physical expression preceded verbal, and, in the most important aspects of life, dominated ceremonial, both sacred and secular. Our own word 'dance' is inadequate to express a range of activity from making love to making war, but 'rhythm', as the word is used above, comes closer to what I mean. Cats dance, birds dance, as does the human being in trance or in mourning. Dance for the Greeks covered almost any activity, public or private, solitary or communal, which required physical expression. Dance was before language and after it, and it could be instead of it. To understand Greek culture, and tragedy as part of that culture, it is necessary to accept that in many walks of life, the physical still dominated the verbal. The progress of Athenian democracy shows men attempting to adjust this priority through the exercise of 'reason'. *Logos*, the 'word', is also 'reason'. What else was democracy but the living proof that argument was superior to force and that the free expression of ideas was what made the Athenian system superior to that of barbarians? The fourth century BC was characterized by philosophers and orators. Tragedy was in decline because the word was dominant. The plays of Aeschylus, of Sophocles and Euripides show speech and picture so closely interwoven that one should not be projected without the other. At points of crisis, however, the words often become subordinate. Characters may revert to lyric metre at moments of crisis. They heighten the language but they dance their grief. And, as I hope to show in succeeding chapters, the moods are displayed as they are described. The relationship between the visual and the aural was constantly explored by all three tragedians. It was their means of expression, bound both to the conditions of the theatre setting and to the masked performance of chorus and actor. But the nature of this performance was rooted, I believe, in a far earlier tradition of story-telling.

The poems of Homer are the earliest Greek literature. A formal text was written down no earlier than the sixth century BC, at least two centuries after they are thought to have been composed and only then in order that sections could be recited at the new festivals created by Pisistratus. They were created in the hexameter metre to be read out by a single reciter, or rhapsode, who could have demonstrated some, though not all, of the qualities of an actor years before the dramatic form proper made its appearance. About the only information we can glean about the rhapsode comes from within the poems themselves. Both *Iliad* and *Odyssey* feature a bard as part of any civilized household of substance. The nature of the material that this bard sings or recites on domestic or formal occasions can be traditional or topical, as is proper in the Homeric world where heroes mix freely with gods and goddesses whose private warring mirrors that of Greeks and Trojans.

The Homeric bard is principally an entertainer, employed to tell stories and valued according to expertise in so doing. Some of the stories are serious, some scurrilous. If his audience laugh at a comic tale, or are gripped by a stirring adventure, then that shows him to be a good bard. In the *Odyssey* Demodocus, at the court of Alcinous, receives such praise from Odysseus that he feels 'divinely inspired' to tell another tale, only to tell it with such verve as to send tears coursing down Odysseus' cheeks and to get himself peremptorily packed off by the host for upsetting his guest. Here in the oral tradition of epic story-telling lies the

germ of the first actor. It is a secular tradition and though the
origins of tragedy have regularly, from Aristotle on, been taken
to reside in some form of religious ceremonial, I suggested
earlier that the secular influence may have been every bit as
potent. This is not to deny the way in which dance formed a
major element in all forms of religious and non-religious
activity, or to underestimate its primacy in the Athenian
theatre.

The Aristotelian view of tragedy was that it had its origins in
a cyclic, non-dramatic dance, the dithyramb, when the group
leader asserted his independence and set up a dialogue between
himself and the other members of the chorus. Later critics have
disputed the details, but most have based their own theories on
a refinement of this relationship between first actor and chorus.
My own belief that actor and chorus were at all times independent is founded on the balance between choral performance and
acting performance. If the story-teller or bard became an 'actor'
by virtue of assuming an identity different from his own, then
'epic' became 'dramatic' at the point of impersonation. That is
the major step forward for which Thespis, rightly or wrongly,
was later given the credit. But what of his relationship with the
chorus and their function in the drama?

When the bard is featured as a character in Homer he sings his
songs as a soloist, but not necessarily in isolation. Demodocus
in the *Odyssey* accompanies himself on the lyre, but is himself
joined in his performance by a group of dancers: 'And around
him the young men gathered, all skilled in the dance, and beat
the floor with their feet, filling Odysseus with amazement at
their movements. Soon to his playing the bard added his fine
voice singing of the loves of Ares and Aphrodite' (Homer,
Odyssey, VIII, 262–7).

Though this may be a surprise to Odysseus it does not seem to
be exceptional as a style of performance. The decoration on the
shield of Achilles described in Book XVIII of the *Iliad* includes a
picture of dancers whirling in and out among the spectators
while the bard is singing, and, as it appears, supplying the dance
tempo.

If this is indeed a pattern in early story-telling with one man
speaking or singing, while simultaneously a group are dancing
around him, it gives at least substance, if not authority, to the
proposition that a major function of this chorus was to supply a

visual dimension through dance to the story-line of the bard.
And when the bard becomes actor and puts on the mask, so do
the chorus put on masks and thereby maintain their prime
function. Certainly this makes intelligible the awkward
remark in the later writer Athenaeus who quotes one Aristocles
as having stated that 'the dancer [or "choreographer"] of
Aeschylus, Telestes, was such a craftsman in dancing [or
"choreographing"] that he made the action apparent simply
through dance' (Athenaeus, *Deipnosophists*, I, 22a). So good
was Telestes, it seems, that even the words were unnecessary.
It makes sense too of the notes by two later scholiasts attached
to texts of Aristophanes. Alongside a passage in *Clouds* we find,
'They used the term "to speak to chorus" when, while the
actor was reciting, the chorus *were dancing the speech*' (my
italics). There is a further note to a text of *Frogs* defining the
word *emmeleia* as 'tragic dancing with the refrain, but some say
the accompanying dance to the speeches'. These two references
are reinforced by the later use of the term *huporchema* to
describe a 'pantomimic' dance.

The virtue of this simple suggestion that the relationship
between actor and chorus in early tragedy was a natural development of that between bard and dancer is that it fills in some of
the gaps left by other theories of the origins of tragedy and posits
a secular performance tradition as influential as the religious
line of Dionysiac festival. It shows why it should have taken so
long for the 'invention' of the first actor (*c*.532 BC) to be fully
explored dramatically before Aeschylus came up with a second
actor at least thirty years later, and Sophocles a third sometime
in the 460s. As G.F. Else first proposed, the second actor was
not brought into use as a source of conflict instead of the
chorus, but to develop the scope of the plot by introducing a
whole series of outsiders to feed new information.[7] The chorus,
once they have arrived on stage, usually stay and are consequently ineffective in promoting the plot. So what was their
function during that long period of time between Thespis and
Aeschylus? Surely they were not simply passive spectators who
sang and danced only when the single actor stopped. The dramatic variations on that formula could have been exhausted in

7 *The Origin and Early Form of Greek Tragedy*, Cambridge, Mass., Harvard
   University Press, 1965.

no time. No, they were dancers whose performance was an integral, vital and infinitely variable part of the entire drama, a graphic function which they were to maintain in part, I believe, throughout the fifth century. Complementary performance of actor and chorus provides the real key to Greek tragedy on stage.

Nothing survives from the tragedies with a single actor, which, if Aristotle can be taken to be reliable in this at least, held the stage until Aeschylus increased the number of actors from one to two. If these early tragedies consisted of little more than the occasional monologue interspersed by choral interlude, their loss seems of small account except to the historian. How much more likely that early tragedy made use of a chorus whose nature was malleable, able to sustain the personality of its individuals as well as to demonstrate a corporate identity of mood? Would not this provide a more solid base from which the genius of Aeschylus could take wing? Even a written text, had one survived, or indeed existed, would be little help and further speculation might show a diminishing return. What we should do instead is look forward to the plays of Aeschylus to see, if at all possible, how the tradition of dance mingled with the oral tradition to supply the pattern of stage performance.

If any store can be set by the impressions of the later classical authors Lucian and Athenaeus, Greek dance was classified into specific dances of which the *emmeleia* and perhaps the pantomimic *huporchema* were examples, and a large number of *schemata*, or figures, which identified sequences of movement for the display of prime emotions. The attitude of supplication by grasping the chin and knees was a *schema*, as was the tearing of cheek or hair in grief. Other *schemata* were less precise and provided a notation, somewhat as in classical ballet, for the choreographer to employ in combination. It was certainly within the capacity of the Greek audience both to appreciate the quality of dance and to follow its meaning. Much of what Athenaeus has to say about individual steps may not have been true of the theatre of Aeschylus, but we would be foolish to disregard his assumption that, first and foremost, the chorus were dancers.

The *schema* could also describe a particular kind of dance. Lillian B. Lawler, whose work on dance in the Greek theatre provides the most refreshing of insights into the possibilities of

Greek tragedy and comedy in performance, identifies the *schema* of 'rowing' to which Athenaeus refers with appropriate choral passages from all three tragedians.[8] Elsewhere images of flying or of riding, of earthquakes and storms, give the range if not the detail of the choreographer's art. And if the chorus danced not only during the choral odes, but also during the dialogue and set speeches of the actors, the visual possibilities of the theatre open out. The messenger who related the off-stage action may have had his words fortified by mimetic or atmospheric movement from the chorus to amplify his own stance and gesture. Cruelty, deception, conflict, reversal, recognition, all the elements of the dramatic scene, have their equivalent in the ever-present chorus. The chorus had special group *schemata*, the actors individual ones. The term *cheironomia* is not found before Lucian and Athenaeus, but the verb from which it comes is used in classical literature to describe the action of someone who gesticulates graphically, not least in Herodotus' story of the tactless Hippocleides who danced away his bride by standing on his head on the table of his prospective father-in-law and indulging in *cheironomia* with his legs. An *a fortiori* case can be made out for a complete system of *cheironomia* being in use in connection with formal Greek dance, and, more particularly, forming part of the actor's equipment: a vocabulary of conventional gesture which could be recognized and understood by his audience. The process of passing from posture to posture then becomes the basic means of communication for the actor. His acting grows out from the mask, rather than being subordinated to it and his relation to objects becomes all the more crucial. The chorus, perhaps, inherited a technique of *cheironomia* from the actor rather than feeding it to him. This would certainly place the emphasis of performance where it should be, on the actor, complemented and reinforced by the chorus.

All this may suggest that acting in the time of Aeschylus was of a formality unfamiliar in the west, though the only kind of stage acting to be found in Kerala or Java. It is certainly a far cry from the 'immovable faces' and 'petrified suffering' which constituted Mantzius' understanding of Greek acting and allows

8 *The Dance of the Ancient Greek Theatre*, Iowa City, University of Iowa Press, 1964.

for the mobility of body in relation to the externals of the stage, as well as the large range of activities and emotions the actor was called upon to demonstrate.

Vase-paintings show that the classical actor of the fifth century BC wore a mask that was simple rather than grotesque, that he wore stage costume appropriate to his station or circumstance and was boosted by neither padding nor high-soled boot. When, centuries later, the tragic actor did sport exaggerated features, the reason is likely to have been connected with the sheer scale of the stone theatres built in the late Hellenistic and Roman periods, against which the human figure could have looked insignificant. Paradoxically the actor probably increased in size as the chorus forsook the *orchestra* and left it for an audience which could now approach the stage more closely. The height of the stage was increased to accommodate the actor and the actor himself was forced to increase his stature in order to be seen from the *orchestra* as much as ten feet below him.

None of this was necessary for the Athenian actor of the fifth century BC and, though costume and mask were clearly intended to make him stand out against the background, the action required in the extant plays is at odds with an actor whose movements were hampered by what he wore. This must remain an area of speculation rather than fact and there is always some doubt attached to scrutinizing surviving texts for evidence of implied movement and business. So often, however, do the texts draw attention to the physical conditions of the stage that we can make an educated guess about both action and reaction from what the characters say.

A large proportion of all entrances and exits were made along the *parodoi* to the far left and right of the acting area. At a conservative estimate the actor had some fifty feet to cover between first becoming visible to a section of the audience facing him and reaching a centre-stage position. Comments from other characters to the effect that a new arrival has been spotted telegraph these entrances and allow up to eight lines before the newcomer speaks. Sometimes it is less, but dialogue and situation dictate the pace. Old men move slowly, messengers sometimes run, choruses often enter in disarray which would simply not allow for the formal entrance formation implied by some later commentators. Within the action characters variously embrace, sink to the ground, writhe in pain, hide and commit violence on themselves or on other people. None of these actions would be out of the question for an actor in elaborate costume, particularly when so many characters have attendants to fetch and carry for them. It *is* hard to believe that the playwrights would have been at such pains to emphasize stage moments which arise out of the actor's mobility if they were writing for actors whose physical aspect was restricted. This is not begging the question, as I hope to show when considering the conscious theatrical sense of each of the tragedians. It is an observation based on the fact that Aeschylus, Sophocles and Euripides each had a highly developed but individual approach to the stage picture, as each brought an individual vision to the stage conditions within which he worked.

In addition to the more obvious movements implied in the texts, there are enough examples within any play of action and reaction for it to be possible to build up a comprehensive picture of the Greek actor's performance. At its most basic this is no more complicated than taking a line such as 'Why do you turn your head away?' and reading into it, not merely the reaction from the person addressed to justify the remark, but an initial move from the speaker to provoke the move away. This is one of the features of acting in the mask. It is not usually a solo process. Acting of any sort requires that the person addressed listens to, or perhaps refuses to listen to, what is being said and shows by his response his attitude to the speaker. Acting in a mask requires more.

Because the masked actor cannot rely only on his face to portray emotion, but must find a total physical expression to amplify his words, so the other members of a stage group cannot listen impassively without nullifying the statement of the speaker. In a mask impassivity is active, not passive. This is not to suggest that the person addressed need be as mobile as the speaker, but it does imply that at any moment within a performance of an Athenian tragedy the stage picture was composed of the physical postures of all present. Indeed this may be one of the reasons for the playwrights restricting themselves to a limited number of speaking characters in any scene, even though an extra non-speaking actor may be present. The sense of composition in vase-painting, whether or not connected with a play, is built round a total tableau and the scenes of action have the peripheral figures in complement to the protagonists. In the conditions of the Greek theatre the playwrights were as confined by what the eye of the spectator could encompass as were those who fashioned friezes by the triangular pediment of the Greek temple.

The actor's performance was itself a kind of dance, a dance in which the main gist of the words was reflected visually as it was sung or spoken. The actors spoke one at a time but the physical presentation was multiple and encompassed anyone else present who could hear and might be affected. This is the basis of the triangular scene used to such an extent by Sophocles, in which the single pronouncement produces contrasting reactions in two listeners. When this sense of action and reaction is considered against the added dimension of a masked chorus, able to act and react both as individuals and in a corporate identity, or as a mirror of mood, the mask can be seen as a device which frees the playwright rather than restricts him and contributes a whole level of meaning not possible in the unmasked performance. Whether the chorus habitually spoke in unison or with the leader speaking for all, either in dialogue interchange with the actors or in the choral odes, is impossible to discover. The chorus frequently makes use of the first person singular in both dialogue and lyric, but there seems little to account for the decision to use the singular or the plural in any passage beyond metrical convenience. Singular and plural would appear to be interchangeable except when a chorus member is speaking as an individual as opposed to a part of his group. When, for example, in the *Agamemnon*, the chorus hear the murder being committed off-stage, they advocate different courses of action. Then they do speak as individuals in the first person, emphasizing that they are at that moment primarily citizens of Mycenae. Such personal moments are not common in any of the tragedians' work but are reserved for strong effect. For the most part the very fact that the chorus can speak of themselves in both singular and plural form strengthens the sense of a corporate nature. It is just as possible that all spoke in the singular as that one spoke in the plural on behalf of the others.

Though it would be helpful to be able to discover some kind of pattern of speech, no convincing one has been forthcoming and it can be no more than personal preference to suggest that the leader usually spoke alone. The rest of the chorus would then have been thought of almost exclusively as dancers. The division of choral ode into *strophe* and *antistrophe* neither strengthens nor weakens the argument, for each semi-chorus could have had its own leader, making two speakers rather than one.

All this relates back to the stage setting and the manner in which the human figure could present himself in space, a sense of which was a part of the visual tradition of fifth-century art. For the most part the actor was seen against a vertical background and the chorus against a circular floor. This depended to some extent on lines of sight and the proximity of chorus to actor, but each of the tragedians seems to have had an awareness of the potential of such a distinction.

The scenic facade of Aeschylus may not have been so different from that of Sophocles or Euripides, but the plays of Aeschylus do contain a greater sense of integration between actor and chorus than is to be found in the latter part of the century. It does seem likely that this was to a great extent a mark of Aeschylus cutting his dramatic teeth on the more restricted use of actors and a more stylized use of the stage. It is quite possible, for instance, that to the Athenian who regularly witnessed plays the most noticeable change as the century progressed was in the externals of the performance. The performance of the actor begins with the mask, but the definition of emotion through gesture is directed by such things as the hang of the costume and the manner in which it presents the human shape. Costume may not have been enhanced by padding, or the mask by the high headdress of Roman times, but there is a difference between the ways in which Aeschylus, Sophocles and Euripides draw attention to what the characters are wearing. Later authorities, dubious though they may be, attest to a grandeur of costume in Aeschylus which there is no good reason to doubt, but the vicissitudes in fortune of Xerxes in *Persians* or the disguise of Pylades and Orestes in *Libation-Bearers* do appear to be introduced by Aeschylus in such a way that the audience would have their situation constantly in mind. Against this is the attitude to Euripides we find in Aristophanes' reference to Euripides having dressed Telephus in rags in his play about that king's fall from high estate. Nor can we deny that Euripides constantly emphasizes the plight of Menelaus in *Helen*, shipwrecked wearing only a piece of sail-cloth to cover himself. Did Aeschylus have such a respect for rank that he identified royalty by rich costume, whatever the circumstances? Did Euripides move so far towards realism that his characters wore what you would have expected them to wear in everyday life in Athens? Are we to consider that the 'rags' of Menelaus meant that the audience saw a figure completely naked except for the remains of a loincloth – and a mask? And what of the marooned Philoctetes with the gangrenous foot and Heracles dying from the poisoned shirt sticking to his back, stage creations of Sophocles?

The answer to all these awkward questions seems to lie in a generalization about how the theatre works. There are certain conventions of the stage which seem to be common not only to the theatre of Athens, but to that of most subsequent periods irrespective of playing-place, occasion and even cultural context. This is a claim too large to consider in any detail here, but it implies a balance between the various features of performance by which the theatre brings together language, literary value, aesthetic appreciation, philosophical and religious speculation to create something which transcends all of them by direct communication between one group of people and another.

Good playwrights share the ability to express the complex through the simple. The stage confines and condenses. Human experience may be funnelled down to a single family, or even one man. Situations can be refined without being devalued. Image is essence. The blinded Oedipus sees what sighted he overlooked. Understanding comes through suffering. Appearance is deceptive. So much that language alone can only reduce to the cliché can gain depth from the example on stage. The stage language of Aeschylus, Sophocles and Euripides incorporates the conditions of performance in Greece. Of these, the size of the theatre and its open-air setting, the sense of occasion and the didactic purpose are the elements which varied least during the fifth century BC.

What did vary was the nature of the experience each playwright wished to transmit. This above all accounts for the differences between them and makes it possible to suggest how they emphasized their individuality within a common theatrical framework.

Aeschylus was more revolutionary, or at least more progressive than Aristophanes gives him credit for when he sets him up against Euripides as a character in *Frogs*. It is the fate of the progressive to pass from fashion when no longer alive to retaliate. A drama as lively as the Athenian remained vibrant by virtue of innovation. To this extent the fourth century BC, by relying so heavily on revivals of plays by the dead Euripides, guaranteed the decline of tragic drama. On the other hand comedy, which in the fifth century was topical, quickly dated but was reanimated by the new social direction it took.

In the theatre of Aeschylus the spectators witnessed the unfolding of a drama which matched the majesty and superhuman qualities of the heroes with a means of performance which enhanced this stature: not literally, but figuratively, so that, despite a simple plotline and characters of restricted subtlety, the drama itself never seems either simple or unsubtle. Occasionally more homely characters tap into the immediate experience of the audience. Often the chorus will demonstrate the consequences of mighty events upon the more humble bystanders, but the major momentum is derived from major issues. So Aeschylus uses strong but accessible effects. He uses colour, he uses pomp, he uses dance, he uses conflicts rooted in the most basic human emotions. He is a poet of 'spectacle' in that his plays, as I hope to show, are built around a single central image, echoes of which reach out in all directions.

Sophocles is an 'easier' playwright, though this does not necessarily mean that he is simpler. There is a sophistication in his symmetry which is often thought of as a direct reflection of the Athenian artistic sensibility. It is perhaps more in his stress on man, the individual, that he reflects the temper of his time. For the chained Prometheus, the wreck of Persia or the fall of the house of Atreus preserved only by Athenian justice, which are the stuff of Aeschylus, Sophocles offers the despairing love of the gullible Deianira, the stubborn individualism of Creon and Antigone or the personal tragedy of Oedipus, undermined by factors beyond his control but destroyed by his own personality. In Sophocles objects have a stage life according to who is handling them and how. A poisoned robe, a bow or a blind man's staff become at moments the entire drama. The characters reveal themselves by the way they relate to their surroundings. Sophocles does represent a move towards humane drama.

The more recognizably human sentiments in his language may well have permitted, or even required, a less formal kind of vocal and physical delivery. The action is swifter, more elaborate. Plays are longer and choruses shorter. He uses more characters and exploits their use in a greater variety of scenes. All of which suggests that the actors probably spoke faster and that this fluency was matched by freer movement, especially as Sophocles so often draws the attention in and focuses it on a central feature. A Sophocles play offers a contrast in pace which contributes to rhythm and to tension. It is Sophocles above all who writes parts for actors.

If Sophocles wrote great parts, Euripides expected more of his actors. The actor in a Euripides play was often faced with having to deliver a line whose subtext contradicted the words. Euripides' characters reveal themselves by what they say, but just as much is indicated by what is said about them. They are more devious in deceit, less self-aware than former heroes. Though it is clearly anachronistic to psychoanalyse an Admetus or a Pentheus, there can be no denying the wealth of subtle reference in the commonplace utterances which typify Euripides.

Yet the actors performed Euripides in the same acting area and to the same huge auditorium as they did Sophocles. The features which today seem most artificial in the Greek theatre were exploited by Euripides for the contrast of convention and sentiment which most marks his individuality.

All three playwrights, then, used the theatre in full knowledge of what contemporary performance would add to their words. The details of staging and costuming can only be hinted at as part of a general principle and the questions about what the Xerxes of Aeschylus or the Telephus of Euripides actually wore in the first productions are never going to be answered. What we can do is uncover the visual imagination of each playwright and at least make some assessment thereby of the theatrical sense of the audiences at various times during the century when theatre flourished. From this examination it will, I hope, become clear, at least in general terms, what was and was not possible in performance. We may never be able to recreate the *Oresteia* or *Oedipus Tyrannus* but we will be able to get far closer to the contribution the Greek tragedians made to an art form which is by its very nature ephemeral.

PART II
THE PLAYMAKERS

5

AESCHYLUS

As the first tragedian any of whose plays have been handed down to us, Aeschylus has sometimes had to run the gauntlet of those who see in the progenitors of any new artistic movement something unformed, if not uncouth. Even Aristophanes, writing *Frogs* little more than fifty years after Aeschylus' death, knew that it was good for a laugh that his stage Euripides should complain of 'all that rugged grandeur' in his rival's work. But it would be entirely wrong to apologize even for the earlier plays we have on the grounds that poor Aeschylus was so primitive that he knew no better. There were plenty of playwrights presenting at the Great Dionysia, both during Aeschylus' youth and later in competition with him, whose work perished without trace. If Aeschylus endures, albeit represented by a handful of seven plays from which only one group of three is effectively complete, we would be foolish to assume that any of them do not survive on merit as some of the best pieces created for the Athenian stage.

What I should like to do at this point is follow through the implications of the performance pattern I posed earlier by testing it against those seven plays. By investigating the manner in which Aeschylus integrated his choruses into the action, it should be possible to see how their presentation was able to reflect a central visual theme in each play.

Because of its episodic nature, with passages of dialogue intercut by choral ode, all Greek tragedy tends to proceed by fits and starts. Even in the more dramatic scenes the action may sometimes be suspended for a time, only to erupt into sudden and violent incident once again. In *Agamemnon* Cassandra's vision, which not even the Chorus can comprehend, occupies a full 250 lines, more than the entire trial scene in *Eumenides*. Sophocles' *Electra* offers a more extreme example. The tutor who brings false news of the death of Orestes in a chariot-race has to convince Clytemnestra of the truth of his story. His speech describing the race lasts all of eighty-three lines. An exciting set-piece in itself, it far outlasts the immediate requirements of the plot. The theatrical effect, dominating the speech itself, resides in the contrasting reactions of Clytemnestra, who is relieved but cannot openly show it, and her daughter, Electra, whose last hope rests with Orestes. The last eighty-three lines of the play contain the entire scene with Aegisthus, from the moment the Chorus set eyes on him through the macabre exhibition of the body under the sheet, the 'unmasking' of Orestes and Aegisthus' own death.

Such contrasts are a standard part of any dramaturgy since, but in Greek tragedy alone is there a chorus geared to unifying the stage action, action to which they contribute, but which proceeds in a different plane from that of the plotline. Even when Sophocles and Euripides had reduced the number of chorus lines to a quarter of the total from the half in much of Aeschylus, it was still the chorus, I would submit, to whom the audience naturally looked to maintain a proper performance rhythm.

In the choral odes of Aeschylus, which are longer and denser than those of Sophocles and Euripides, the images are often specific. In *Seven Against Thebes*, for example, the Chorus sing:

> Now, friends, sigh for a fair wind, beating hand on head for the sweep of the oars which sends the black-sailed ship to Acheron, to the shore where Apollo cannot go and where no sunlight falls. (854–60)

Though the directions to a modern choreographer are often less clear than in this passage, the scene or mood is usually specific enough to suggest a framework for the dance. Grief, apprehension or elation are the primary emotions invoked, while more descriptive sections rely heavily on the kind of metaphor which can be easily translated into physical demonstration.

So much is clear. But the choral odes all involve a suspension of direct action. What of the chorus within that action? I contended earlier that the original function of the chorus was to add a visual dimension to the spoken word of the actor. Few would dispute that Aeschylus had inherited and, by the time of the surviving plays, had refined a theatre tradition of telling a story through movement, through gesture, through music and through speech. He had a theatre available which paraded certain physical features and relationships, all of which he could use. He also had an audience familiar with stage performance, and with a changing artistic awareness which permeated their everyday lives, however mundane their occupation. In these factors allied to a developing religious and civic system, there resides all that is needed to uncover in his plays a theatrical technique both immediate and profound.

The breakthrough from seeing early tragedy as part of a simple Darwinian progression from choral to character drama came with the redating of *Suppliants*, the most choral of all the surviving plays, not as an early piece but as one of Aeschylus' latest plays. At the end of his writing career – and the *Eumenides* alone should have prevented it from ever seeming otherwise – the chorus was still for Aeschylus a mobile and tangible force with a variety of theatrical functions.

To see how Aeschylus promotes the medium of theatre through and beyond choral performance, it becomes necessary to consider one or more aspects of each of the earlier plays. Except in the case of *Suppliants* the chronological order of the plays is of only marginal concern in the main argument. It is more a matter of convenience than anything else which dictates starting with *Persians*.

Persians is the only surviving tragedy to deal directly with the recent past of Athens. Set in Susa after the defeat of the Persian army by the Greeks at Salamis in 480 BC, it opens with a Chorus of Persian elders waiting for news of Xerxes' expedition against Greece. The Athenian audience knew full well what the news would be and that it could only bring despair to the Chorus. The Chorus are immediately identified as aliens with alien sympathies, at least in their immediate *persona*, but the anticipation they feel is emotionally keyed to that of the audience. They enter at the beginning of the play and sing an introductory ode in which they set the scene and extol their heroes, but anticipate grief throughout the state should the expedition have met with failure, not success. The first character to appear is the king's mother Atossa, with whose fears they sympathize and to whom they counsel caution.

A Messenger arrives and describes the destruction of the Persian forces. Atossa questions him for 250 lines before the Chorus launch into an ode of grief for their country and their countrymen. Before the arrival of the Messenger the Chorus have been fairly animated, particularly in the dialogue with Atossa. Is it possible to believe that the Messenger's famous description of the battle of Salamis was greeted without choral reaction when it is so much in the nature of masked acting for reaction to balance action? At a strictly realistic level this reaction is one of horror, which can for a short time be represented by stillness, but the Messenger's speech is peculiarly graphic. If the imaginative leap can be made whereby the Chorus can at one and the same time be seen to function in the dual role of witness and expositor, then the lines of the Messenger almost come to resemble stage-directions or notes to the choreographer.

> ATOSSA: Your words bring great light to my house, shining day from darkest night. (299–300)
> MESSENGER: Thus did some god destroy the army, weighing down the scale with unequal balance. (345–7)
> Some avenger or evil demon set in motion the entire disaster. (353–5)
> First from the Greeks arose a cry of triumph answered in echo from the island rocks. (390–1)
> The Greek ships circled us and battered us. The sea was nowhere to be seen, blanketed with wrecks and bodies. (416–20)
> The sea was full of screaming and groaning till the scene was hidden by darkness. (426–8)

Some lines imply a direct mimetic response:

> The commanders kept their ships plying to and fro all night. (382–3)

Swiftly they came into view, the right wing leading in good
order. (398–400)

These examples are chosen almost at random, but line after
line conjures up a stage picture where the speech of the Messenger and the reaction of Atossa would be enhanced by the
behaviour of the Chorus. It is only when the Chorus can be
understood to possess individual and corporate identity, tied
impersonally to the structure and rhythm of the play, that the
relationship of actor to audience becomes clear. The *orchestra*
of the pre-Periclean theatre was so positioned, with the audience two-thirds of the way round it, that the Chorus within the
orchestra could function equally as performer or spectator. It is
this spatial arrangement as much as anything which contributed to the Chorus fulfilling the role of intermediaries by
reflecting the drama in their corporate identity at the same time
as being personally involved as interested parties. Few, if any,
later western playwrights have employed such theatrical vision.

The choral ode that follows the departure of the Messenger is
all the more poignant because of the ambivalent attitude of an
Athenian audience for whom the Persian defeat had been a
mighty victory. Grief is usually externalized in Greek tragedy,
though seldom by this sort of paradox. But it is a feature of all
three tragedians that when suffering becomes almost too great
to comprehend, then the tragedians retreat, or perhaps advance,
into formality. Because the actor in a mask has to demonstrate
his feelings rather than indulge in them, set responses of affection or grief are signposted by a series of physical movements.
Extended from the individual to the chorus, this *cheironomia*
allows for an ode both to crystallize the experience of the play so
far and to provide a composite living representation of grief as a
mosaic pattern against the *orchestra* floor.

Prometheus is set in the mountains of Scythia. The Titan
Prometheus, who has defied Zeus by offering fire to mankind, is
punished by being exposed, chained to a rock, with no hope of
escape. There he is visited first by the chorus of Oceanids, his
cousins, who appear to fly in, and then by their father Oceanus,
who claims to be in a chariot drawn by winged horses. Oceanus
is replaced by Io, like Prometheus a tormented victim of Zeus'
cruelty and Hera's jealousy. The last visitor is Hermes, the
messenger god, who warns of the dangers of further opposition

to Zeus. Prometheus remains defiant and Hermes tells the Chorus to stand clear as Prometheus is engulfed by an earthquake.

This is a strange and wonderful play, part of a trilogy of which the rest is missing, but still unlike anything else we possess. No one would suggest that the language in *Prometheus* was originally matched by realistic production with its mountain-top setting and winged cars, but the piece is full of physical descriptions whose very extravagance implies a proper theatrical means of presentation. Strange though it may be the play is not inconsistent and the movement it describes must surely have had some visual equivalent.

The opening of the play does not involve the Chorus at all. Prometheus is brought on by Power and Force, who are directing a reluctant Hephaestus to fasten him to the cliff:

> POWER: Hurry to place the chains upon him lest the Father see you delaying.
> HEPHAESTUS: The manacles are ready as you see.
> POWER: Cast them round his hands. Use all your might to rivet him to the rock.
> HEPHAESTUS: There. The work is done and well done.
> POWER: Harder. Strike harder. He is clever enough to escape the harshest restraint. (52–9)

Nor does it end there. Power continues in the same vein, eventually ordering a wedge to be driven through Prometheus' chest.

Prometheus meanwhile utters not a sound, nor does he speak until Power, Force and Hephaestus have all departed. Left alone, he at last breaks his silence, revealing in his stage position his solitariness. What makes his isolation seem so complete is that Aeschylus has held back the entry of the Chorus. The actual staging has been the object of much speculation from those who define 'the furthest confines of the earth', Power's description of their destination in the play's opening lines, as a large open space, to those who favour scenic representation. For years commentators subscribed to the view that a dummy would have been used for Prometheus, behind which the actor would apparently have stood. This utterly implausible notion has nothing to support it and creates far more problems than the one it arguably solves by having a Prometheus who can have a stave driven through his chest. Far more reasonable is the suggestion that Prometheus was shackled against a scenic piece on an *ekkuklema*. This would certainly ease the ending of the play and seems to be supported by a later vase 'almost certainly stage-inspired', as T.B.L. Webster described it, depicting Prometheus fettered to his rock.[1]

What is important is that even the least probable of these solutions does not affect the theatrical point. During his first speech Prometheus is seen to be alone. The Chorus come to him during that speech, but this Chorus is unlike any other in Aeschylus. To begin with they have barely a fifth of the lines, whereas other choruses in Aeschylus have up to half of the total. Their prime function, however, is quite in keeping with the relationship between other choruses and the main actors. Indeed it is an advance in one respect. The Chorus of Oceanids who arrive 'with racing wings' and 'free as birds' arrive in order to *dance* that very freedom of which the hero is deprived. After their initial exchange with Prometheus, he invites them 'to descend to earth'. This may imply that by some strange contrivance they were introduced above the actor, but even were this no more than a figurative reference – the play is not short of parallels – it is not fanciful to see the remark as an invitation to them to become dancers and assume the regular role of a chorus.

From this point onwards, and the play is already a quarter done, this is what they do. They give way to new characters played by a second actor, and in a partial paradigm of the development of the tragic form, release themselves for this primary purpose. Oceanus in his chariot, Io persecuted by a gadfly which allows her not a moment's rest or respite, Hermes with his winged sandals, all these characters demonstrate the mobility which Prometheus does not possess. The Chorus were assumed to be dancers and through the rest of the play they dance, inspired by the characters' descriptions of the hundred-headed Typhon, of Atlas, of flight and dreams, of flowing rivers and exotic lands, of Gorgons and Griffins.

Inevitably the Chorus must be part of Prometheus' fate. Hermes pays little attention to them until warning them to

---

1 Trendall, A.D. and Webster, T.B.L., *Illustrations of Greek Drama*, Oxford, Phaidon, 1971, p. 61.

stand aside before the earthquake overwhelms the Titan. It is Prometheus who then commentates on his own fate, perhaps as he is finally withdrawn inside the *skene*. But that part of the staging is less significant than the rest of the picture. Surely what happens during that climactic speech of Prometheus is that the Chorus *dance* the earthquake, clearing the *orchestra* in their headlong flight and leaving Prometheus once more alone.

Seven Against Thebes, dealing as it does with an incident within the story of the House of Laius, offers an informative point of comparison between the dramatic methods of Aeschylus, Sophocles and Euripides in handling myth. The Aeschylus play deals only with the circumstances of the deaths of Eteocles and Polyneices, the two sons of Oedipus, who fall out over who shall govern Thebes. The rest of the trilogy is missing.

The first line of the play has Eteocles addressing Thebes: 'Citizens of Cadmus, it is now the task of the city's guardian to say what must be done' (1-3). Unless the main characters simply walked into position, the play must have opened with Eteocles making an entrance, but what of the citizens of Thebes? They could be the Chorus entering from the opposite side, but the Chorus do not speak until line 78 and their first words are uttered in panic at the approach of war. The Chorus are also described as *parthenoi* or 'maidens' and, flexible or not, this Chorus does not seem to provide adequate representation for the entire citizen body.

Most translators, faced with supplying stage-directions to make some sense of the action, favour the entrance of a crowd of citizen extras, who promptly go off with Eteocles just before the Chorus come on. This is hardly a satisfactory staging sequence if the choral entry is to follow immediately, and along the same *parodos*. A modern director would surely opt for Eteocles addressing the real audience. It can often be inappropriate to apply the techniques of modern production to the classical theatre, but Aeschylus is here concerned to engage the attention of the Athenian spectators and focus it on a state of war with which his audience would be only too familiar. When the Chorus do appear the lines suggest a state of panic: 'I utter cries of terror. The army is let loose. . .who can save us?' (78-9; 91). They can hear, they say, the clatter of hooves, the clang of shields, the rattle of ten thousand spears, chariots and heavily loaded axles, the air whirring with the vibration of lances, stones showering on the parapet. The audience need hear nothing at all, though a modern audience would expect a confused noise even if they could not identify each and every sound. Do the lines not serve equally as a guide to the choreographer? Much of the sound and certainly the resulting sense of panic could be created vocally and physically, by stamping, clapping, beating the mask. One phrase stands out in this context. At line 103, the Oxford Text reads *'ktupon dedoika'*, 'I fear the noise'. The original manuscripts are unanimous in reading *'ktupon dedorka'*, 'I see the noise'. *Vix credibile*, adds the critical apparatus, dismissively, but *'dedorka'*, 'I see', is perfectly acceptable. When a scene is created on stage, as Aeschylus creates scenes, the din of battle is concrete, something to be shown and seen. The audience do *see* the terror of the Chorus, the chaos of impending battle as well. The Chorus are not only objects, affected by fear, they are agents through whom the fear is given form in the eye and mind of the audience.

Now these three plays have the common feature that the Chorus of each is in a position, not only to watch the action and to comment on it, but to contribute to the audience's view of it. They also have another feature in common, one that is perhaps less a matter of speculation than the nature of choral dance which is ultimately unknowable. It is still an aspect of theatrical imagination and, as such, is curiously overlooked. *Persians*, *Prometheus* and *Seven Against Thebes* are all constructed around a single visual image of extraordinary power and significance, an image that stems directly from the graphic nature of the Chorus.

In *Persians* the image is one of grandeur brought low. Every emphasis is placed in the early part of the play on the pomp of the Persian empire. The glory of the force that set out is described in detail, the elders who comprise the Chorus are finely dressed. And consider the first appearance of the Queen, as she arrives from her golden palace and the Chorus catch sight of her:

> Here, shining like the eyes of the gods, comes the mother of the King, our Queen. I make obeisance before her. (151–4)

As the play proceeds the vision of invincible power is gradually whittled away. Atossa, the focus of attention while the

Messenger reveals the extent of the disaster, is steadily reduced. Her second entrance, 'without my chariot and my former finery', shows her humbled, while the ghost of Darius, the former king, itself serves as a reminder that the glory of Persia is a thing of the past, a wraith without substance or hope. The concluding scene spells out the full extent of the cataclysm by centring on the person of the defeated Xerxes. His entourage is minimal, his chariot a decrepit reminder of Atossa's carriage. Piece by piece he displays the marks of defeat, the torn robe, the empty quiver. Together the Chorus and the king hopelessly support one another in a dirge. In terms of recognizable stage action, little happens in *Persians*. Theatrically it is still potentially a *tour de force*.

Prometheus most obviously marries poetic theme with stage picture in the contrast between the immobilized central figure and the restlessness of those who interrupt his solitude. The image is not simple. Prometheus is the immortal who has dared to help mankind in defiance of Zeus. His ultimate gift was the forlorn one of 'wan hope', but first he gave men fire, itself a metaphor for the knowledge that drew man from his primitive state, a metaphor for science, medicine, augury and husbandry. As Aeschylus elaborates on the implications of the myth, so he promotes them through the vision of the chained Prometheus who holds a secret of which even Zeus is afraid. Progress carries a high price, a price which ties man down, but will ultimately bring benefits to make up for the hardship. Reduced to its essence the saviour of mankind is a god chained to a rock, weighed down but defiant. It is as telling a figure as Christ on the cross and as archetypal. Prometheus' apparent helplessness becomes the source of his strength, while what seems to all the other characters to be freedom is a part of their weakness.

Seven Against Thebes, no less than the other two plays makes use of an extended image to promote the whole play. It offers a warning, a warning against the dangers of civil strife. The message is as unambiguous as Norton and Sackville's message to Elizabeth I in *Gorboduc*, the pre-Shakespearean tragedy. The civil war in *Gorboduc* is caused by the failure of the king to ensure the succession. *Seven Against Thebes* offers a warning to the whole of Athens, couched within the myth of the sons of Oedipus, of the dangers to which the squabbling of contemporary politicians Cimon, Ephialtes and Pericles may lead.

The destructive divisiveness of civil strife cannot easily be demonstrated in a play set within the city for which the two parties are striving. Only one faction is properly represented. This difficulty seems to provide a stimulus for Aeschylus as he contrives to construct a stage picture which balances the two sides. By the arrival of the Messenger, if not earlier, the Chorus are split:

> FIRST SEMI-CHORUS: My friends, the lookout brings news, I think, hastening as fast as his legs will carry him.
> SECOND SEMI-CHORUS: And here comes our master, son of Oedipus, at the right moment to hear the Messenger's report. (369–75)

Eteocles must have made his entrance from a different side, presumably the opposite *parodos* from the Messenger. He is accompanied by the six champions, himself the seventh, who will protect the seven gates of Thebes. The audience and the Chorus know that Eteocles intends to fight, but the Messenger was not present when he made the announcement. As each of the enemy heroes is described, Eteocles selects a champion to oppose him. The process is a slow one. Finally only Eteocles is left and the Messenger reveals that his brother Polyneices is at the seventh gate.

A comprehensive sense of symmetry within the play is given its final and most telling visual emphasis with the funeral procession of the two brothers, each slain by the other's hand. The Chorus review what has happened and watch as Antigone and Ismene appear, escorting the bodies of their brothers. Though the Chorus can sing that the brothers' enmity is at an end as their blood has mingled on the earth, so the image of civil war is at odds with the lines. The picture of a settled Thebes is torn in half as one sister mourns one brother and the other vows to bury the other. The play ends with the unusual and rather shocking sight of the Chorus still divided:

> FIRST SEMI-CHORUS: Let the State take action or not against those who mourn Polyneices. We will go and join in the burial. This sorrow is a common one and what the State deems just can vary with circumstance.
> SECOND SEMI-CHORUS: We will accompany this other corpse as the State and Justice approve. For it was this man,

helped by the gods and mighty Zeus, who saved the city of
Cadmus from sinking beneath an alien horde. (1067-78)

Suppliants, for so long supposed to be an early play, is far
easier to assess in the light of such a performance tradition. If
the first actor developed alongside but independently from the
chorus, rather than as an offshoot from it, the choral nature of
Suppliants is immediately intelligible. The Chorus of daughters of Danaus, who have fled to Argos to avoid an unwanted
marriage, feature as the central element in the drama. The play
opens with their entrance and the first actor does not make an
appearance until line 175. In only one short passage does one
actor address another directly before the confrontation between
King and Herald. This confrontation lasts little over fifty lines
and the last hundred lines are again dominated by the Chorus.

Accepting that *Suppliants* is a late play, perhaps the latest of
Aeschylus' plays to survive apart from the *Oresteia*, we must
look at its form with care. This is not the fledgeling work of a
man who later learned how to do without so much chorus, but
the conscious attempt of a working actor/playmaker to expand
the possibilities of the theatre within an established framework. The overall design is unfortunately difficult to decipher
in a trilogy, two parts of which are missing. That the trilogy
dealt with questions of alliances and the rights of the individual
makes it likely that, at the time of first performance, it had as
much application to contemporary Athens, and indeed Argos,
as did the *Oresteia*. That *Suppliants*, even taken in isolation,
has a corresponding theatrical force can only be shown if it is
accepted that the Chorus may be used as a powerful descriptive
weapon within any scene in the play. Their dual purpose is even
more significant when their real *persona* is the main driving
force of the play. They have an identity as the fifty daughters of
Danaus and apparently their hand-maidens. This 'real' personality is only one part of their nature. At the same time as
promoting the central action of the play, the Chorus serve to
amplify it. They are both representatives (of the hundred
women) and demonstrators of the action. The manner in which
Aeschylus manipulates their speeches to make this dual function possible, sometimes within the same sentence, marks a
considerable feat of dramaturgy and an imaginative leap that
looks forward as well as backward.

This is the first extant chorus central to the stage action. Much of the choral response in *Suppliants* is in dialogue form, spoken perhaps by the Chorus-leader alone, and illustrated by the others. But when the King sees his predicament, fearing to turn away the suppliants, fearing no less to incur the wrath of the Egyptians, it would have been well within the convention for the Chorus also to reflect his dilemma. Personal concerns feature largely among the remarks of the Chorus, but despite their extravagant grief the mood of the play as a whole is one of tight restraint. The outburst of violence by the Herald and his soldiers is all the more outrageous as a contrast, one of a series of contrasts that Aeschylus builds into the play.

When Danaus first arrives, he advises the Chorus to take sanctuary:

> It is better, daughters, to seat yourselves at this mound of the assembled gods. An altar is stronger than a tower. (188–90)

The statues of several gods are mentioned individually and seem to be visible as, in a later moment of real shock, the Suppliants threaten to hang themselves from them.

The Chorus dance the first ode in the *orchestra*, but then, on Danaus' advice, cluster round the altar. This altar appears to be a scenic piece. Once 'in sanctuary' it takes a specific guarantee from the King to get them to return to the *orchestra*.

> CHORUS: What am I to do? Where will I be safe?
> KING: Leave your branches, token of distress.
> CHORUS: I leave them where you indicate, and as you have said.
> KING: Turn back to the flat space by this grove. (506–9)

The ode that follows this unusual focus on the place of sanctuary is full of violent language as the Chorus sing and dance the story of Io, the same Io who has featured as a character in *Prometheus*. When the Herald is seen approaching with soldiers, they probably return to their former position of sanctuary. The sense of shock that they feel when the Herald tries to drag them away is mirrored by theatrical shock at the rupture of familiar convention. Though violent action is quite common in Sophocles and Euripides, it occurs infrequently in Aeschylus. However literally or otherwise we interpret the cries of the Suppliants, 'He is dragging me off like a spider', and however quaint their complaints sound, 'He holds me like a snake and bites my foot', the barbarism of their oppressors is clearly established.

The involvement of the Chorus in the physical action of the play is a considerable advance on their interpretative function in works considered previously, though it is to their former role as the embodiment of the stage action that they return in the concluding lines of the play.

This Chorus of *Suppliants* emerge as a concrete demonstration of the family group, united in corporate action, but alive to their own individuality. They are able both to pattern the action of the play and bring a personal response by being physically threatened as real people. Here we have no return to a primitive dramatic form but an enhanced use of a theatrical device belonging to a high art. It is appropriate that *Suppliants* should now seem to be late Aeschylus because the handling of the chorus looks directly towards the *Oresteia*.

The *Oresteia* is the summation of Aeschylus' work as a man of the theatre. At one level the progression of the chorus from *Agamemnon* through to the *Eumenides* reflects the elevation of the conflict from the human plane to the divine, but within each of the three plays the contribution of the Chorus is calculated with scrupulous care. The Elders of *Agamemnon*, too old to go to war ten years before, serve as a reminder of the weakened state of Argos. No sooner do they take off into a choral ode, however, than they become visionaries, possessed of information and an ability to interpret it that could not be sustained by their surface identity.

This clearly presented no difficulty for an audience familiar with Aeschylus' dramatic method. They do not so much change identity as demonstrate their basic nature, which is to amplify the play at more than a single level of understanding. One of the great set-pieces of all Greek tragedy is Clytemnestra's beacon speech in which she describes how she knows of the fall of Troy. The speech is framed by remarks from the Chorus made as loyal subjects. But this is no obstacle to their dancing a speech which is virtually self-contained.

In the *Agamemnon* the Chorus effect little. They hint, they warn, they observe, they reflect. But when Cassandra reveals her knowledge of events to come, there is no possibility of the

Chorus understanding what she is talking about. Through most of the play they speak with a single voice. At the moment when Agamemnon's death cries are heard from indoors, there is the sudden twelve-way split as twelve individuals voice their reactions to what they hear:

> My advice is summon the citizens here to the palace.
> Mine to rush in and catch them sword in hand.
> I say we must do something together. No time to delay.
> It is clear. They mean to set up a tyranny.
> We're wasting time. Their hands do not slumber in caution.
> I know not what to advise. The man of action should be the
>   planner.
> I agree. How will we bring the dead to life with words?
> Do we submit to tyrants to prolong our own lives?
> Never. Death were better than tyranny.
> Are we to believe our master dead on hearing groans?
> We should find out for sure. Surmise is no proof.
> Do we not all agree we must find out the truth? (1348–71)

This sudden fragmentation combines superbly the very human reaction of a group of frightened men with a deeper sense of the dissolution of the state itself. Even so, or perhaps because of the physical break-up of the group, the Chorus achieve little beyond vilifying Clytemnestra and uttering vague threats against Aegisthus' soldiers.

To say that this Chorus effect nothing is not to suggest that their part in the play is a minor one. Even in the later plays of Euripides, in which the odes have sometimes only the most tenuous connection with the plot, the contribution of the Chorus to the whole play is considerable.

In *Agamemnon* a new facet of behaviour is introduced, the dramatic significance of which may be overlooked because today we take it so much for granted. At the end of the 'beacon' speech Clytemnestra prays for a safe return for the soldiers:

> May no impulse fall upon the soldiers to destroy what they
> should not, overcome by greed. For a safe journey home they
> must complete the return trip. (341–3)

This is the first speech in the surviving tragedies in which a character says one thing meaning something else.

Clytemnestra is speaking 'in deceit' and the audience are aware of the fact only from their prior knowledge of Agamemnon's homecoming as a familiar piece of history or myth. One wonders, however, whether this deceit might not have received special emphasis either vocally or, more probably, physically in the actor's pose and gesture while the words were delivered. Would it not be likely that a dramatic device which comes to be used so regularly, and may indeed have already been familiar before the *Oresteia*, would be signalled by some figure understood to be a part of the *cheironomia* employed in all masked drama and dance? And might not this too have been reflected through the Chorus?

If a single character aims to deceive others in *Agamemnon*, in *Libation-Bearers* the entire Chorus, slaves hostile to Clytemnestra, provide the turning-point in the play by an act of deception. Established as friendly to Electra and her brother, the Chorus witness the recognition scene and hear Orestes' plan to gain admission to the palace in disguise. The plan works and Orestes is invited inside. At this moment Aeschylus introduces a most telling stroke. Out from the palace comes Orestes' old Nurse, herself a slave. A beautiful little scene reminds the audience witnessing mayhem among princes, that, amidst such grand passions, the love of a nurse for a child can be more sincere and more touching than all the accumulated hatred. The Nurse has several dramatic functions. She clears up any lingering doubts that Clytemnestra's reaction to the news of the death of Orestes might be taken at face value and offers a contrast in love to the real mother as she recalls her devotion to Orestes as a baby. She also has a job to do. Clytemnestra has told her to go and fetch Aegisthus. The Chorus are sympathetic, but not to the extent that they are prepared to reveal their own privileged knowledge. They simply tell her to change the message so that Aegisthus will come to the palace alone. As individuals they are privy to the plot, and thereby take part in it, but they are still canny enough to take no real risks until they are sure whose side to be seen to take. To Aegisthus they merely state, 'We did hear, but go inside yourself and learn from the strangers. No messenger's report makes up for first-hand knowledge' (848–50). When they in their turn hear the screams from indoors they react as plausibly as their counterparts in *Agamemnon*:

How goes it? What has been decided in the house? Let us
stand aside so as not to appear to be accomplices in evil-
doing. The outcome of the battle has been decided. (870-4)

Only when they can see the bodies there in front of them are
they prepared to admit their relief at the outcome. By showing
the Chorus becoming involved with the progress of the plot, but
at the same time making sure they are not implicated if things
go wrong, Aeschylus makes them a major focus of dramatic
action. As long as the audience can *see* that the Chorus are
uncertain, the outcome remains unpredictable. By a nice stage
paradox the move into realistic behaviour allows them to function more completely at a symbolic level.

In the last play of the trilogy the Chorus not only affect the
plot. They dictate it. They give the play its title and they are at
the heart of what is perhaps the most remarkable *coup de
théâtre* in all Greek drama. That moment depends upon a
visual build-up which Aeschylus prepares throughout the
trilogy by means of a series of striking theatrical devices.

As we know from later writers Aeschylus was renowned for
the spectacle in his plays. *Persians*, however, as we have seen,
is built around the image of splendour diminished and it may
well be that in *Agamemnon* the King's entrance, delayed as it is
until half-way through the play, is less grandiose than some
commentators would have us believe. Apart from its symbolic
level, the shipwreck described by the Messenger who precedes
the King has the purely practical purpose of accounting for
the fact that Aegisthus is not immediately deposed by
Agamemnon's army. If Agamemnon's retinue consists only of a
small escort who leave the scene as soon as he retreats into the
palace, then there is no one *except* the Chorus to draw sword
against Aegisthus' men. Agamemnon, for all his regal appearance, has been in every way debilitated by the ten years of war.

Agamemnon opens with a Watchman waiting for a beacon to
light up, the sign that Troy has fallen. The device of setting the
scene for a tragedy by introducing a minor character was, of
course, to become a familiar one in the sixteenth and seven-
teenth centuries. This Watchman is at pains to rehearse to the
audience his grievances until the scene is established and he
sees the fire blaze out. The notion that the play would have
opened just before dawn so that the rays of the sun would strike
the *skene* on cue is perhaps a fanciful one, but it seems to be the

sort of effect that would have appealed to Aeschylus. As H.D.F. Kitto pointed out, the image of light and enlightenment is one that recurs throughout the trilogy right up to the torchlight procession which concludes the *Eumenides*.[2] There is, of course, no need for a real beacon and the Chorus express themselves sceptical of its significance. Dramatically the beacon gives Clytemnestra time to complete her preparations and allows the Messenger, who arrives later, to offset the triumph of Troy with the realities of warfare. The way is paved by Aeschylus for Agamemnon to appear, rather less impressively than his position as commander of the conquering army might have led the audience to anticipate.

When Clytemnestra at last confronts her husband the stage picture is particularly forceful. Agamemnon presumably arrives with Cassandra, driven in his chariot up the *parodos* into the *orchestra*. Clytemnestra is in the dominant position by the central door facing down towards the *orchestra*. Clytemnestra's long speech of greeting is delivered with the other major figure in the scene, Cassandra, still and silent, and concludes with the following words:

> Now, dear lord, dismount from your chariot, but do not place your foot upon the ground, conqueror of Troy. Servants, why do you delay, whose job it is to strew the path with tapestries? Spread scarlet on his way to the house he never expected to see. Justice dictates it. My unsleeping mind will arrange everything else fittingly as the gods ordain. (905-13)

Agamemnon is apprehensive and a battle of wills ensues, Clytemnestra's proving the stronger. Agamemnon concedes:

> If you think so, well. Let someone quickly loose the shoes which enslave my feet. And as I tread let no envious eye be cast upon me from the gods. It is shameful for my feet to mar the household wealth of woven work. (944-9)

After a further soothing speech from Clytemnestra Agamemnon walks on the red carpet up to the palace. Agamemnon, the victor in a cruel war, whose triumph has entailed the sacrifice of his daughter and the slaughter of countless of his subjects, now paddles home along a river of blood pouring from his own front door.

2 *Form and Meaning in Drama*, London, Methuen, 1956.

Cassandra is left behind and to emphasize the isolation of the victim of Apollo, whose full understanding of the situation divorces her from the other characters, Clytemnestra returns in a second attempt to entice her into the palace. Only when Clytemnestra has once more returned indoors does Cassandra utter her first words. What the audience have seen has been a solitary, still figure decked out in the emblems of prophecy, the robe, sceptre and garlands which she herself now rejects:

I destroy you before I destroy myself. To oblivion. I trample upon you. (1266-7)

This scene with Cassandra is no afterthought. The stage properties have a specific function in reminding the audience of the role played by certain gods within the play. Cassandra makes her own way into the palace stripped of all the features which marked her as a representative of Apollo.

Similarly, in *Libation-Bearers* the function of Pylades, who has only three lines in the whole play but is Orestes' constant companion, becomes clear in performance when his physical presence can never be taken for granted. When he does speak, the audience is surprised perhaps that he speaks at all. But on the one occasion when Orestes' resolve flags, Pylades is there to remind him of Apollo's warning.

In *Agamemnon*, when the bodies are revealed, Cassandra is lying beside Agamemnon, though exactly what was shown in the original performance is not clear. As Clytemnestra describes the murder she threw 'an evil wealth of robe' over Agamemnon and caught him 'like a fish in a net'. Aegisthus talks of Agamemnon 'lying in a robe woven by the Furies'. The robe is stained with blood, the same colour as the carpet. There is even blood on Clytemnestra as the Chorus note 'the remains of blood on your eyes'. The tableau remains until the very end of the play and the robe itself in which Agamemnon was entangled is used again in the second part of the trilogy.

All the most dramatic moments of the *Agamemnon* are given visual reinforcement. The same is true of *Libation-Bearers*, in which special emphasis is placed on comparisons.

A notable example of stage awareness occurs in the recognition scene. Orestes arrives with Pylades and pays homage to his father's tomb by placing a lock of his hair upon it. Seeing Electra and the Chorus approaching, he withdraws until sure of his reception. Electra catches sight of the hair and compares it with her own, discovering that it matches in texture and colour. Then, seeing footprints, she places her own feet in them and discovers that they match as well. Orestes emerges from hiding and puts paid to her lingering doubts over his identity by showing a piece of cloth she wove for him as a child.

Fifty years later Euripides was to 'send up' the scene when he had his Electra jeer at the old shepherd for suggesting that brothers and sisters might have the same colour of hair or size of feet, or that a shirt might grow with its wearer. But it is Euripides who is at fault here in failing to appreciate Aeschylus' 'recognition' on its own terms as stage device. Electra places the hair from Orestes against her own, and it does not matter whether the audience can even see the hair. The recognition is the gesture. She places her foot in the place where the audience has seen Orestes stand. And the echo suffices. The cloth clinches it, not because Orestes is still wearing it, but simply because Electra recognizes it. The echoes are echoes of stage position, of posture and behaviour. The complexity of allusive and poetic image in which the *Oresteia* abounds, is concentrated in visual stage equivalents.

Contrast works in the same way. The aged Nurse, slow and grief-stricken as she makes her long exit up the *parodos*, believes that her only happiness has been destroyed. Audience and Chorus know the reverse to be true. A choral ode later Aegisthus enters from the same place, the same actor in all probability, forceful, buoyant and elated by the Nurse's news. Quick where she is slow, vigorous where she is decrepit, his reactions are every bit as ill-founded as hers.

When the dead bodies of Aegisthus and Clytemnestra are revealed in *Libation-Bearers*, the tableau has been prefigured in the *Agamemnon*. The setting for *Libation-Bearers* has the tomb of Agamemnon as a central feature. So little notice is taken of it in the latter part of the play that a change of location has been suggested by some critics. The tomb is only referred to as it features in the action when Electra offers her libations, or Orestes and Electra pray for success. As the plot against Clytemnestra develops, the practical value of the tomb disappears. It is no less important, however, for it still to be visible as a constant reminder of the reason for Orestes' vengeance on his mother. As such, it serves to counterpoint the figural significance of the corpses on display, sealing the revenge.

Even richer in significance is the robe of Agamemnon which Orestes brings in:

> Now, see, you who hear of these evils, the device which fettered my wretched father, binding his hands and feet. Spread it out. (980–3)

Orestes displays it on the ground as Clytemnestra had her servants spread the red tapestries. Then he picks it up again:

> What shall I call it? By what euphemism? A trap for an animal or a shroud? A net, a snare rather to cripple a man. (997–1000)

The blood-red colour, as has often been noted, is featured again when the Chorus blame the blood fresh on Orestes' hands for his derangement, while the Furies, he imagines, 'drip blood from their eyes'.

The link back to the earlier play provided by these visual reminders of Agamemnon effectively ties up the first two plays and prepares the audience for the third. Had only *Eumenides* survived of the *Oresteia* trilogy, it, like *Suppliants*, might have been classified simply as a 'choral drama'. As it is, Richmond Lattimore could write in the introduction to his translation, 'The Chorus has returned to its archaic part as chief character in the drama'.[3] The trilogy seen as a whole shows how lopsided an assessment this is. Aeschylus' central concerns are contemporary to the Athens of his time, to the Council of the Areopagus, all but suppressed in 461 BC, and to the growth of democracy in fifth-century Athens. His themes, religious, political and sociological, are concentrated in the Furies who dominate the action. The description of them is startling enough to anyone expecting a group of loyal citizens or harassed slaves. The Priestess enters on her knees after seeing these 'women, no not women, Gorgons, not even Gorgons. . .wingless, black and foul' (46–8). Apollo describes them as 'ancient children spawned by neither god nor man nor beast', and orders them back to nethermost Hell from which they must have sprung. So vile was their appearance, the late and far-from-reliable *Life* of

---

3 *The Complete Greek Tragedies: Aeschylus I. Oresteia*, trans. R. Lattimore, Chicago, Chicago University Press, 1953, p. 29.

Aeschylus tells us, that pregnant women had miscarriages at the sight of them and little boys died of fright. What Aeschylus has dared to do is to create in concrete stage terms creatures so horrific that normally they lurk only in the deep recesses of man's subconscious. These Furies belong in the worlds of Poe or Lovecraft, a world of nightmare, terror and loathing.

The first entrance of the Furies presents a complex staging problem. The play opens before the temple of Apollo in Delphi. The Priestess who sets the scene retires into the temple, only to re-emerge on her knees to inform the audience of the horrific scene which has greeted her. She leaves for good, perhaps along a *parodos*. Apollo then arrives and speaks of the Furies as though he is able to see them. They are asleep and do not wake up until Orestes, dispatched by Apollo to Athens, has left the scene and the ghost of Clytemnestra has arrived. A scholiast's note suggests that the Chorus could be seen as soon as the Priestess returned from indoors, while the *Life* also says that the Chorus entered 'Sporadically'.

As no *ekkuklema* could be expected to hold Orestes, Apollo and Hermes, who accompanies him, and twelve sleeping Furies, the most satisfactory solution to the choral entrance would entail a small number – two or at most three – of the Furies on the *ekkuklema*, the rest making their entrance one or two at a time when goaded by Clytemnestra's ghost. The real surprise for an Athenian audience could well have been the entrance of any chorus through the *skene*. How far their primeval nature dominated the behaviour of the Furies in the rest of the play is difficult to determine. Despite Apollo's abuse, they offer reasoned argument to both Apollo and Athene. In the trial scene they cross-examine Orestes in a manner almost Demosthenic, but when the verdict goes against them, they revert to their true nature. Here lies the key to Aeschylus' intention in creating such grotesque figures in the first place. In the last sequence of the play Aeschylus uses their hideousness for his most striking effect.

At first reading the *Eumenides* may look unbalanced. The trilogy shows the murder of a husband by a wife, the vengeance of the son on the mother and the son's trial and acquittal. But the trial and its outcome are not the whole of the *Eumenides*. Orestes is not even the central figure, though his acquittal does resolve the curse on the house of Atreus.

The trial is over by line 754. Orestes makes his final exit twenty-three lines later, but the play has almost a third of its length still to run. Indeed the trial, though providing a dramatic climax, does not represent the climax of the trilogy. When the gods have admitted that the case is too difficult for them to resolve, the burden of enforcing the law is returned to mankind, and the jury system is instituted. Twelve ordinary citizens are selected to show how practical democracy may solve any problem, subject always to the casting vote of Athene. Aeschylus has the goddess cast her vote for political growth and the superseding of the old law by the new. But where does this leave the implacable Furies?

The remaining quarter of the play is taken up with Athene's conversion of the Furies from the hideous creatures of the opening to benign deities who will protect the city. From the atmosphere of fear and disgust conjured up by their mere presence in the opening of the play and their rabid fury when thwarted of their victim, Aeschylus contrives a transformation so powerful that at the end of the play they leave the stage in triumph. The conversion is gradual, but there seems to be one particular moment when they accept their changing role.

CHORUS: Queen Athene, what function do you offer me?
ATHENE: One free from all trouble. Accept it.
CHORUS: Were I to accept it, what honour remains for me?
ATHENE: That no house may prosper without you.
CHORUS: Would you help me gain such power?
ATHENE: Yes. We will help the fortunes of the reverent.
CHORUS: And do you give me a pledge for the future?
ATHENE: I will not promise what I cannot fulfil.
CHORUS: You seem to soothe me and my anger departs.
(892–900)

Exactly what stage effect Aeschylus had in mind at this moment when the Furies accept their new role, we can never know. Suggestions have varied from a complete change of both mask and costume to a simple change in movement pattern. Were the sniffing hunters who pursued Orestes so relentlessly to do no more than stand upright the effect could have been powerful, though not in itself sufficient. The whole final sequence, the procession with torches and singing reminiscent of the Panathenaic Festival, must have seemed an uplifting celebration of the city itself.

And here too, dominant among so many examples of theatrical skill, we have the trilogy's entire theme translated into visible form through the medium of the Chorus. Justice *is* the Eumenides until twelve ordinary citizens face the challenge of blind supernatural power, and, by the gesture of casting votes, ensure that change and progress are possible. It may be Athene who weights the balance in favour of Orestes, but it is the twelve silent figures who make her choice possible. And, as the conversion of the Eumenides solves the insoluble problem, the stage picture is transformed into Athens itself, glorious and immediate.

If the refinement of this extraordinary vision could never quite be reproduced in a theatre today, there is no denying a sense of theatre behind the lines of any Greek tragedy which could be comprehensible to a modern audience. But stage technique does not remain static. Sophocles no doubt learned his craft in the Theatre of Dionysus watching the plays of Aeschylus and his lesser contemporaries. When he came to create his own plays, however, he looked not backward to their way of working, but forward to a new exploration of his complex and flexible medium.

6

SOPHOCLES

Sophocles defeated Aeschylus at the Great Dionysia of 468 BC on the first occasion that he competed. For twelve years as a young man he was a rival to Aeschylus in the dramatic competitions and presumably was in the audience at the first performance of all Aeschylus' surviving work. He could not but have been influenced by the innovations in stage technique for which Aeschylus was responsible, but that first victory must have given him the confidence to accept that he could be the one to inherit Aeschylus' mantle and lead tragedy in a new direction.

Not that Aeschylus abdicated at that point, for what we must regard as his greatest work was still to come. But even in the *Oresteia* most of his characters remain larger than life with the chorus usually prominent to highlight and enhance a total view of myth translated into contemporary experience.

Sophocles chose a different path, at least in so far as we can judge from his extant plays, the first of which was not presented until well after Aeschylus' death. Gone are the formal heroes and the panoramic view of the stage. Instead we are introduced to a world of unusual personal detail, a world in which a small object or a human gesture can define a man's estate. There is little attempt to disguise the trials and tribulations of being alive: 'It is best not to have been born at all: but, if born, as quickly as possible to return whence one came'. Such is the philosophy of the Chorus in *Oedipus at Colonus*, the last and as it happens, the most hopeful of all Sophocles' plays. Tragedy, of course, deals in death and disaster, and grief is its keenest emotion, but Sophocles concentrates alarmingly on physical suffering. Crippled Philoctetes, mutilated Oedipus and dying Heracles haunt the stage of Sophocles, demonstrating not the stoicism of mankind but the pain to which he is heir. Mankind for Sophocles is capable of heroism, but for most men the price is too high.

Consequently the theatre of Sophocles is far different from that of Aeschylus. Reputed to have been a wise and kind man in his political and personal life, Sophocles reflects this by engaging sympathies in his writing. His situations and characters are closer to immediate human experience than are those of Aeschylus. Individuals display human flaws and foibles. The choruses frequently have a specific role to play as people no less than in Aeschylus, but Sophocles sometimes seems to justify their existence in a manner which Aeschylus found unnecessary. This is not to suggest that Sophocles made any pretence that a play was anything but a play, taking place in a theatre – this he had in common with his contemporaries – but Sophocles in the best possible way 'exploits' the theatre. His particular contribution to dramatic structure is the staging of conflict, in particular conflict between opposing forces rigid in attitude and uncompromising in action. Accordingly he makes special demands on his actors in terms of the relationship between characters. The sense of balance between opposing views and the effect produced by the presence of a third person reveal an acute awareness of the audience's view of the stage.

Antigone is still regularly revived. The notion of the individual fighting against the gods which gives impetus to Aeschylus' *Prometheus* appealed more to the Romantic period. The individual defying temporal power has a twentieth-century appeal.

The scene is set before the Palace of Thebes. The story of Antigone and Ismene, sisters of Eteocles and Polyneices, is picked up at the point at which Aeschylus left it at the end of *Seven Against Thebes*. The brothers are dead and Creon has decreed that Polyneices shall remain unburied. But where Aeschylus made use of his stage picture to demonstrate the effects of civil war, Sophocles is more concerned with the moral processes of the individual. Dramatically the central issue is revealed with some subtlety. Antigone and Ismene enter together as the play opens. They argue about the wisdom of acting against Creon's decree and then leave separately. The argument is carefully structured and the situation handled realistically. By delaying the arrival of the Chorus, who throughout the play are the advocates of moderation, until the situation is established and the sisters have declared themselves, Sophocles makes it possible for the central argument at the crisis of the play not to involve the sisters at all.

The Chorus comprises Theban Elders who are concerned in the long term, as is Creon, with the good of the state. The argument of the play is quickly diverted from the two girls to the Chorus who contribute few lines to the dialogue, but enough to assert their confidence in Creon's decisive step taken at a time of crisis.

After the first choral ode, during which the Chorus sing of their relief that the war is over, news arrives of the first attempt to bury Polyneices' body. Creon's reaction is fierce but not unexpected. Neither Creon, Chorus, nor Guard knows who has been responsible for what has happened, but in the second ode a note is sounded which anticipates the head-on collision between Antigone and Creon. The Chorus warn of the man who is 'too rashly daring', referring to whoever was responsible for the burial, only moments before Antigone is led in by the Guard. Principal characters usually leave the stage during the choral odes. Antigone and Ismene do so just before the entrance of the Chorus. Creon retires into the Palace before this ode and has to be recalled after it. But from this point in the play when Antigone first confronts him, Creon appears to stay on stage even during the choral odes. He speaks the final words before the third ode and the first words after it, with no suggestion that he has left the scene. In all probability, he did not make an exit until after the Chorus have persuaded him to change his mind, when he sets off, too late, to revoke his decision. In the context of the whole play and the conflict it proposes between personal and public morality, Creon's physical presence at a time when the Chorus would normally expect to have the stage to themselves has a powerful impact. Creon is established as a personal force in his own right as well as a representative of the ruling house. The effect recalls, and is a development from, the 'silent' figure of Aeschylus.

All through the dispute between Creon and his son the Chorus are tactfully subdued. Not until Teiresias, the seer, has responded to Creon's taunts by forecasting further disaster do the Chorus make a stand. Faced with the infallible predictions of the blind prophet they recommend a pardon and Creon retracts. Though primarily responsible for Creon's change of heart, the Chorus then revert to their earlier function and can only serve witness to the rapid sequence of events which follows. As they offer relief at Creon's change of mind, so they reflect despair when he arrives too late to save Antigone or Haemon and then suffers the ultimate blow of his wife's suicide.

In *Antigone*, as in *Ajax* and *Women of Trachis*, Sophocles uses the Chorus to clarify for the audience the attitude of someone indirectly involved. Their attitude is not necessarily that of Sophocles or the attitude he wished to instil in his audience, but their physical position of standing between actors and audience still gives them part of the nature of both. They may have reflected the confrontations of characters: Ismene and Antigone, the Guard and Creon, Creon and Antigone, Haemon and Creon, Creon and Teiresias. This could have been done by division into semi-choruses or by corporate response to each speaker in turn. They might have indicated by physical attitude, gesture and mask the sway of argument between characters, or their own changing attitude to central events. What is difficult to believe is that they would have stood and watched impassively. One of the surprising features of rehearsing a Chorus in a theatre is the way in which movement, far from detracting from the focus of attention, can actually confirm it. The further away the audience sits, the greater the effect. The Messenger speech, delivered to a mobile chorus in Aeschylus, itself seems an inheritance from the dramatic method of the Homeric bard. Hardly a play of Sophocles or Euripides does without a Messenger speech, and even those that do contain at least one descriptive speech of considerable length relating some off-stage incident. It may well be that the later chorus maintained some of its Aeschylean function and provided a visual stimulus during the narrative.

The theatre of Sophocles is less visual than that of Aeschylus.

More subtle characterization demands closer attention to the spoken word, but the relation of speech to stage picture can still be underestimated. Often strong moments involve devices which are part of the stage armoury of any dramatist, ideas already exploited by Aeschylus: the character who speaks in deceit, the words spoken in one sense which the god's eye view of the audience interprets in another, the build-up of suspense, surprise, irony, reversal of expectation, the moment of recognition, the aspect of grief, the excitement of confrontation.

Antigone has several such moments. Creon's sudden capitulation to the advice of the Chorus after refusing to listen to Antigone, to his own son Haemon or the respected prophet Teiresias, is one. The reversal would be inexplicable without Creon's reaction being visible during the 27-line speech of Teiresias in which he threatens Creon with pollution and the death of his son. The speech is provoked by a taunt from Creon about the venality of prophets. But after this scene the Chorus require only three hesitant lines for Creon's resolve to crumble. This is psychologically sound as long as the speech of Teiresias is *seen* to be as effective as he means it to be. It also ties in ironically with the earlier lines during which Creon forfeits any sympathy he might have enjoyed from an Athenian audience:

CREON: And was she not defiled by lawlessness?
HAEMON: Thebes is unanimous in denying it.
CREON: Is the city to tell me what to do?
HAEMON: Do you not see it is you who sound naïve?
CREON: Do I rule this land for other people or for myself?
HAEMON: A city for one man, is no city. (732–7)

Two individual moments in the play exemplify Sophocles' consistent reinforcement of dramatic highlight with a visual effect. The first occurs during the second and final meeting of Antigone with Ismene. This is our first example of a Sophoclean triangular scene. Ismene refused initially to help with the burial of Polyneices. When Antigone is caught, Creon accuses both the sisters and immediately Ismene confesses, though her presence in the palace belies any involvement. Antigone reacts with a certain pique. Creon suddenly finds himself standing between two sisters fighting as only sisters can for responsibility for an act which he has announced as a capital crime. Hardly surprising that he ends the exchange with the line 'I do believe the creatures both are mad', as near as Sophocles ever comes in his tragedies to a comic moment.

The final view of Creon is particularly striking. He is the man who has tried by whatever means to restore sanity after the havoc produced by the other members of the family of Oedipus. But he is just as much a part of the house of Labdacus as they are. After only 580 lines of the play Ismene leaves the stage and does not return. Antigone departs to her death after line 943. Haemon's body is brought back on stage, to be joined by that of his mother Eurydice who has killed herself at the news.

The reasoning behind this is theatrically powerful. For all that the play takes its title from Antigone, it is Creon's immediate family who are destroyed. They are destroyed by Creon's folly, though his fault is human enough. The curse on the house of Oedipus is something that neither Laius, Jocasta, Oedipus nor his children can dodge. Beyond universal Fate there is a personal fate that each man makes for himself. The rigid man, proud and solitary, who remains on stage during the choral odes and Antigone's lament, is the same man who is brought low by nothing more sinister than his own unyielding nature. At the end even Antigone is forgotten as a man mourns the death of his wife and only son.

Ajax cannot be firmly dated but is usually regarded as an early play. The plot concerns the madness and suicide of the hero who was defeated in the competition for the arms of Achilles. It begins with the victor Odysseus being told by the goddess Athene how she prevented the Greeks from being murdered in their tents. This opening is quite unlike that of any other surviving play of Sophocles. The first character the audience sees is Athene, the only occasion on which Sophocles introduces one of the Olympians into a play. Her first words are addressed to Odysseus:

> Son of Laertes, I have watched you trying to gain some advantage over your enemies. Now I spy you at Ajax' tent at the end of the line by the ships, scouting, measuring his tracks to see whether or not he is inside. (1–7)

Odysseus, who is presumably in front of the *skene*, cannot see Athene, who is presumably on top of it, nor does he throughout the scene. Athene tells Odysseus that Ajax has made an attempt on the life of Agamemnon and Menelaus but that she has driven him mad so that he has slaughtered a flock of sheep and cattle believing them to be his human enemies, and is at that very moment torturing more within the tent. To Odysseus' dismay she calls Ajax outside and taunts him. Ajax returns to his tent and Athene boasts to Odysseus of the power of the gods. Odysseus replies:

> Enemy though he is, I pity him, bound to an evil fate. There, but for the grace. . . We mortals, I see us as shadows, nothing but a shade. (121–6)

To which Athene quickly replies:

> Let such a sight be a warning to you never to speak against the gods. (127–8)

This is an extraordinary scene, partly because charity is the last quality which the dramatists usually allow to Odysseus, partly because of the sheer cruelty of Athene, who is, after all, the patron goddess of Athens. That humanity should be the prerogative of a human character rather than a god is not in itself unusual for Greek tragedy. The gods tend to display a cool indifference to human feelings and this is the last place for a Christian conscience. It is still strange for Athene to gloat over human fallibility, so much so that it is more than tempting to look for a personal statement by the playwright on the need for compassion within the state of Athens. Perhaps the 'theology' of Sophocles consists neither in approval or disapproval of the gods, Athene in particular, but rather in a sympathy for mankind whose godlike strengths can so often prove weaknesses in the stony face of Fate.

Soon after the arrival of the Chorus of sailors, Ajax is shown again amid the havoc he has wrought. As John Moore wrote in the introduction to his translation of the play, 'The disclosure of Ajax in his tent, fouled by the animals he has insanely tormented and killed is more than a powerful *coup de théâtre*; it is a fearful and summary image of total degradation not merely of heroic, but of all human, value. The process by which this image is transformed and Ajax' disaster irradiated by his recovery of heroic strength and human relatedness is the true action of the play'.[1]

---

1 *The Complete Greek Tragedies: Sophocles II. Ajax*, trans. J. Moore, Chicago, Chicago University Press, 1957, p. 3.

This obscene tableau remains in view until it is withdrawn, probably at the end of the ritual lament. Such is Ajax' shame that Tecmessa and the Chorus are fearful for his safety and more immediately for that of the child Eurysaces. Tecmessa confronts him with the child and, in a touching moment, Ajax gives the child his enormous shield before returning inside. Tecmessa and the child are left at the door while the Chorus sing a choral ode about the downfall of the hero.

When the ode is complete Ajax returns, his mood changed. He seems calm and clear-headed when he announces that he will go and cleanse himself in the sea. His final remarks serve to reassure both Chorus and Tecmessa: 'When next you hear of me, though now I suffer, I will have been freed' (692). The exultant dance of the Chorus, who believe that Ajax has recovered from the disaster, serves only to increase the apprehension of an audience who realize that Ajax' pride in himself has been destroyed.

This is a particularly good example of the theatrical device of contrasting stage picture with the audience's understanding. Sophocles promotes the device and proceeds to build upon it. A Messenger arrives warning of the hostile feelings towards Ajax' brother Teucer among the rest of the Greek army. There has been a prophecy as well. If Ajax can last the day, all will turn out well. Teucer has sent instructions that Ajax should stay indoors. But Ajax has already left. Tecmessa then asks the Chorus to go and find Ajax and all those on stage exit – Tecmessa, Eurysaces, the Messenger and the entire Chorus.

This is not necessarily the only time in surviving Greek tragedy that the Chorus leave the stage in mid-action. It may well have happened in Aeschylus' *Eumenides* and Euripides' *Alcestis*. As in *Eumenides* the scene changes, here to the seashore, a location which could have been represented easily enough by change of emblem. But Ajax reappears alone, left to carry on the action entirely single-handedly.

Carefully and deliberately Ajax sets up the circumstances of his own suicide during a speech of over fifty lines. Sophocles uses the calm of irrevocable decision on numerous occasions within his plays and always to increase the audience's awareness of climactic events. Ajax, witnessed only by the audience, an Athenian audience attuned to the Chorus as perpetual witnesses to major dramatic events, falls on his sword. There could be no more powerful stage image of despair.

The Chorus arrive, perhaps split into groups from either *parodos*, in search of their leader, but it is left to Tecmessa to discover the body and inform the Chorus that Ajax is dead.

Of all the arguments which suggest that the Chorus were personally involved in the main action rather than being considered as bystanders to be switched off when not speaking, none is stronger than the need Sophocles felt to remove the Chorus at the moment of Ajax' suicide. It would have been simple enough for Ajax to have killed himself inside his tent during a choral ode and for his body to have been presented, as were the bodies of the slaughtered animals, on the *ekkuklema*. Sophocles intends this death to remain fixed in the mind of the audience for the rest of the play. The body remains in full view, the subject of a wrangle between Teucer and Menelaus, until carried off in procession at the very end. The physical presence of Ajax, even when dead, dominates the play in a way that the physical remains of Polyneices never feature in *Antigone*. In this dead figure Sophocles concentrates the major theme of the play.

Odysseus finally persuades Agamemnon to let the corpse of Ajax be buried. Odysseus has not appeared since the prologue, but only during his defence of Ajax does it become clear why it should be Odysseus who opens the play with the 'invisible' Athene. Odysseus is regularly portrayed in Greek literature as guileful and full of deceit, a man who thinks more than is good for him. Because he has talked to Athene, a goddess he cannot see, and borne witness to her lack of humanity, Odysseus is in a position to suggest that Ajax was not responsible for his actions. Athene herself becomes a metaphor for a mental affliction and Odysseus, the most attuned of the heroes to the subtleties of the human mind, becomes the apologist for Ajax's temporary insanity. It is a skilful device contrasting the seen and the unseen in a manner which Euripides was to develop in plays such as *Hippolytus* and *Bacchae*.

Women of Trachis is a much underrated play, perhaps because it suffers from a similar production problem to *Ajax*. The central character, Deianira, wife of Heracles, leaves the scene and kills herself with a third of the play still to run. Most of the rest focuses on the agonized Heracles writhing in the poisoned robe sent to him by Deianira in the hope of recapturing his love. In *Antigone* the name character quits the scene before the important issues have been resolved, but neither she nor Deianira, nor indeed Ajax, are weakened as characters because of it. Indeed there is a strength in Deianira which makes her plight as moving as anything in Sophocles.

The play opens with Deianira lamenting the constant absence of her husband while she is forced to make her home among people she does not even like. Were it not for the series of fears which torment her, the first speech might bear comparison with the comic opening of Euripides' *Helen*. But Deianira's innocence is much more vulnerable than the charming naïveté of Euripides' Helen. When she invites her son Hyllus to go and look for his father, Hyllus already knows where he is and why: 'The rumour is that he has been a slave to some Lydian woman for the last year' (69–70).

Deianira has received an oracle that Heracles will either meet his death in Euboea where Hyllus says he now is, or will survive to live a peaceful old age. When Hyllus hears this he agrees to go and look for Heracles. The Chorus are sympathetic to Deianira and encourage her to talk about her love as she unfolds the intensely personal tragedy of a woman of rare gentleness in a world of monotonous barbarism.

Innocent though she may be, Deianira is far from stupid and when a Messenger arrives with news of Heracles' imminent return, she is suspicious that the Herald Lichas has not yet arrived in person. When Lichas does turn up, he has with him a group of women captives and tells Deianira that Heracles will return as soon as he has fulfilled a vow made in the country to which the captives belong:

DEIANIRA: By the Gods, who are they? Who do they belong to? They're pitiable unless their present state deceives me.
LICHAS: When he sacked Eurytus he chose these for himself, and for the Gods.
DEIANIRA: Was it to capture that city that he stayed away such a countless length of days?
LICHAS: No. Most of that time he spent in Lydia, by his own account no free agent, but enslaved. No reason to be ashamed, my lady, when Zeus contrived it. He was enslaved to Omphale, the barbarian queen, for a whole year, as he himself admits. (242–53)

Lichas' somewhat tentative account conceals the fact that he is holding something back and, if Deianira does not know the whole truth, then, unusually for Greek tragedy, neither do the audience. Lichas is deceiving her, though she accepts his version of events, being distracted by pity for one captive in particular:

Poor girl, who are you? Unmarried? A mother perhaps? To look at you you seem inexperienced, though nobly born. Who is she, Lichas? Who are her parents? Tell me. I pity her most of all for she alone seems aware of her position. (307-13)

Lichas hedges, revealing only that the girl has refused to speak since being taken from her home. As he takes the prisoners away the original Messenger, who has been listening to what they have said, draws Deianira to one side and informs her that Lichas is a liar:

I heard him say, and there were plenty of other witnesses, that it was because of this girl that your husband laid low Eurytus and high-towered Oichalia. Love, alone of the Gods, spurred him on, nothing to do with the Lydians or Queen Omphale. (351-6)

The 'year of slavery to a foreign queen' had been enough to rouse Deianira's fears, but this is much worse, especially when the Messenger reveals that the girl is Iole, daughter of Eurytus, brought back as a Cassandra to live with Heracles. Quickly she summons Lichas and in an elaborate triangular scene, Lichas blusters about the difference between truth and gossip. For the most part it is the Messenger who challenges Lichas, but Deianira is the focus of attention. The truth is painfully extracted, but by this time Deianira and the audience realize what is going on.

When Deianira finally does speak, she admits, in a speech of simple dignity, that this is not the first time that Heracles has loved other women. Lichas, shamed, confesses to what really happened and apologizes for the lies which were his own invention and not instigated by Heracles.

This still, dignified figure, silent while the men wrangle, demonstrates a romantic love unusual in Greek tragedy. Here we have no Clytemnestra or Medea, whose destructive passions can only respond with blood, but a woman, the gentleness of whose nature prevents her from demonstrating anything but love and compassion. All she wants is to win back her husband's affection and the charm from Nessus seems the obvious way. As she offers to Lichas the robe, impregnated with the Centaur's blood, to carry to Heracles, the entire conflict between affection and passion, between love and hate becomes crystallized in this crucial stage property.

Lichas exits with the robe intended to rekindle love, only for Deianira to discover that the mixture has disintegrated the wool with which she applied it to the robe. In this violent male world innocence can only be destructive. The arrival of Hyllus confirms her worst fears. Here again, as we have seen in *Antigone* when Creon changes his mind and when Eurydice resolves to kill herself, the important decisions are made at a time when the audience can see them, but when another character is speaking. Deianira is no less the focus of attention than Hyllus as he gives details of what happened to Heracles when he put on the robe. In the last few lines Hyllus turns on his mother:

> Such things did you plot against my father and bring to fruition. May Justice and the Fury make you pay. So do I pray if it is right, and it must be right, for right is what you have overthrown, laying low the best of all possible men whose like you will never see again. (806–12)

Deianira makes no reply as a guilty woman most surely would. Instead the Chorus supply the action: 'Why do you creep away in silence? Do you not know that silence strengthens your accuser's case?', threatening their own position as sympathetic friends.

As the Nurse later reports it, Deianira moved from room to room in the house, touching familiar objects. Then she made up her husband's bed before impaling herself on a sword. Greek drama offers no more touching portrait of a loving wife.

The arrival of Heracles, still stuck to the poisoned robe, introduces the final section of the play in which Hyllus, aware now of the injustice of his accusations, tells the dying Heracles about his mother's good intentions and Heracles, resigned at last, makes his funeral arrangements. Over-prolonged in the reading, this section, as so many others, depends upon a visual image. The robe, 'an ensnaring net woven by the Furies', as Heracles describes it in a phrase which echoes the description of the coverlet thrown over Agamemnon, is melting into Heracles' skin. Offered and received as a mark of love, the garment clings to the hero and will not let him go until it has destroyed him. Once Deianira has left the scene, the robe remains to remind the audience of the love that brought down a hero as none of his enemies could.

No reliable date has been suggested for *Women of Trachis*, but it is generally thought to have been fairly late. *Oedipus Tyrannus* probably preceded *Women of Trachis*, but despite the gap of over twenty years between the two Oedipus plays, it is convenient to consider the *Oedipus Tyrannus* in tandem with *Oedipus at Colonus*. This leaves *Electra*, most plausibly dated to just before the Euripides version of 413 BC, and *Philoctetes* reliably dated 409 BC.

Sophocles' version of the Electra story covers the central part of the Oresteian trilogy of Aeschylus, as does Euripides' *Electra*. The Sophocles version is plainly Sophocles, the playwright basing his treatment of the myth on a single dramatic twist. Whereas in Aeschylus' *Libation-Bearers* and Euripides' *Electra* the murder of Aegisthus precedes that of Clytemnestra, Sophocles makes it his climax. The difference in emphasis is apparent from the opening. Orestes arrives with an old Tutor, the man who rescued him as a child. There is no Pylades, and Orestes and Electra do not meet until the last third of the play. Instead Sophocles offers a level of moral conflict, similar to that of the *Antigone*, in the person of a sister Chrysothemis, whose function resembles that of Ismene. Electra's isolation from family and friends is staged in a similar way to that of Creon by leaving her on stage from the moment she first appears. In one marvellous effect, however, Sophocles shows complete originality.

Because Clytemnestra is killed first, and with the minimum of fuss, there is little of the moral tension over the question of matricide which pervades the versions of the story by Aeschylus and Euripides. Instead Sophocles offers a revenge drama, the conclusion of which contains the most glorious moment of pure theatre in all Greek tragedy. Aegisthus is away from the palace when Orestes arrives bringing an urn in which he claims to have his own ashes. News is sent to Aegisthus only that

Orestes has been killed and his body returned to his home. Orestes duly dispatches Clytemnestra without much fuss and prepares for Aegisthus. Expecting to gloat over the corpse of his stepson, Aegisthus is presented with a figure under a sheet. He asks Orestes to lift the coverlet. Orestes says that Aegisthus should lift it. Aegisthus agrees, pauses, asks for Clytemnestra. Orestes tells him she is close by, and Aegisthus lifts the shroud, revealing, not his enemy, but his wife. For the progress of the plot no more pointless confrontation could be imagined, but it is this moment which lingers in the mind and helps distract an audience from the uncomfortable issue of matricide with which Sophocles prefers not to deal.

To suggest that Sophocles side-tracks his audience from paying too much attention to an aspect of his theme which he has failed to develop fully, is not to offer an apology for weak construction. Sophocles was particularly skilful in steering his audience along paths he wished them to tread without allowing them to become diverted. The dispute between Electra and Chrysothemis over how they should react towards their mother compares with the feud in *Antigone* between Antigone and her sister over the burial of Polyneices, but is no mere copy. *Electra* is self-contained and has a happy ending. True, Chrysothemis is introduced to provide a contrasting point of view as to how her sister should behave, as is Ismene in *Antigone*, but Chrysothemis has a much more important function in isolating Electra until Orestes finally reveals himself. Though the circumstances of the play render the act of murder morally correct, the treatment she has suffered has turned Electra into a recognizable daughter of her mother. The three-handed scene in which the Tutor provokes, by his false story of the chariot race, contrary reactions in mother and sister of the 'dead' man is a classic use of the device. In itself it justifies the extension of the descriptive speech far beyond the immediate requirement of convincing Clytemnestra that Orestes has been killed.

Sophocles is particularly adept at 'zooming in' on a small action or object which contains a core of action for the play as a whole. The 'urn' scene in which Orestes offers Electra proof of his own 'death' is a cogent example of Sophocles' use of a physical property to highlight emotion. When Orestes arrives on the scene, after the Tutor's long descriptive speech about his supposed death, he brings with him, as he and the Tutor have agreed, an urn. Electra has no doubt that the remains of her brother are inside. Orestes is now in a dilemma. He does not at this stage wish to reveal himself even to his sister, but his resolve wavers when faced first by the moving lament she addresses to his 'ashes', and then by the gradual realization of her appearance and what she has suffered physically and mentally by keeping faith with his memory.

A long passage of *stichomuthia*, line-by-line dialogue, follows between them during which all grief and hope become focused on this single object, the urn. For each it means something different. They pass it from hand to hand. Orestes cannot face being so callous as to leave her unhappy. Gently he leads her to realize that this property, which symbolized the death of her hopes, is in reality the opposite. By means of the urn the two are united, even though the plot against Aegisthus and Clytemnestra is nowhere near complete. Their joy is so unconfined that the Tutor has to rush out from the palace to warn them to be quiet before someone hears.

Philoctetes offers a similar sequence in which the 'zoom lense' of Sophocles concentrates the attention onto a single object at a moment of crisis. Part of a prize-winning group at the Great Dionysia of 409 BC, *Philoctetes* provokes mixed reactions today. It is not easy to find sympathy for a tragic hero marooned on a desert island because his foot smells. Not only are we never allowed to forget the pain Philoctetes is suffering, but in a moment which, had it been created by Euripides, would seem like self-parody, Sophocles has Neoptolemus discover Philoctetes' infected bandages hung out to dry.

All the same the play's moral has a contemporary ring and in the realism of staging and language shows Sophocles apparently influenced by the Euripidean method. The opening of the play emphasizes the theatrical nature of the setting. Odysseus and Neoptolemus enter, presumably up the *parodos*:

ODYSSEUS: This is the beach of the island of Lemnos, untrodden by man and uninhabited, Neoptolemus, son of Achilles. (1–3)

Odysseus then tells Neoptolemus to look for a cave with two entrances and a spring:

NEOPTOLEMUS: Lord Odysseus, this is a brief quest. I think I see the cave you mean.

ODYSSEUS: Above or below? I do not see it.

NEOPTOLEMUS: Up there, but there is no sound of footfall.

ODYSSEUS: Look and see if he is asleep.

NEOPTOLEMUS: I can see his dwelling is empty.

ODYSSEUS: Is there any sign of domestic comfort?

NEOPTOLEMUS: A few leaves, strewn for a bed.

ODYSSEUS: But nothing else, no other indication of life?

NEOPTOLEMUS: A hand-made wooden cup of poor workman-
ship, and a bit of kindling.

ODYSSEUS: And these are household treasures! (26–37)

What the audience actually saw as the setting for this play is
something else, of course. There is no reason for thinking that
the set was constructed within a different convention to that of
other plays of the period. Indeed Odysseus and Neoptolemus
are at such pains to point out how lonely and primitive the cave
is that their description would seem superfluous were the audience presented with a realistic representation. If the standard
skene was employed, perhaps with *paraskenia* for the two
entrances rather than a central door, then the setting could
easily have been identified by emblems painted on the panels,
with the dialogue supplying the detailed touches. The bedding,
cup and firewood are all inside the cave, though the rags to
which Neoptolemus subsequently refers would seem to have
been visible. That Philoctetes' washing-line should be a prominent feature of a Sophoclean setting seems incongruous at best,
but Sophocles does use his physical effects with care. It may be
that Sophocles wished the audience to be constantly reminded
of Philoctetes' affliction, just as the presence of the bow serves
as a reminder of Philoctetes' value to Odysseus.

Inherited from Heracles this bow has a double dramatic purpose. It is the weapon which Odysseus needs to steal if Troy is
to be defeated. But he is also afraid that Philoctetes will use it
against him if he recognizes him. The bow is missing when
Odysseus and Neoptolemus first search the cave. Philoctetes
never goes anywhere without it and, from the moment he
appears on the scene, Neoptolemus' entire energy is directed to
gaining possession of this vital weapon. Neoptolemus deceit-
fully gains Philoctetes' confidence to the point of asking to see
the bow. Philoctetes says that he may, only for Neoptolemus to
hesitate, torn between old loyalty and new. As Oliver Taplin

pointed out, this gives the bow a moral significance.[2] More than that it shows, as does Orestes' urn in *Electra*, how the conflict and issues of a play become concentrated in a stage piece and who is addressing it. This is a stage world whose significance Samuel Beckett has most fully exploited in our contemporary theatre, but there is no major dramatist who has failed to take some account of it.

The Chorus of sailors are a party to the deception planned by Odysseus. They witness the whole transaction and, as Neoptolemus accepts Philoctetes' invitation to enter the cave, they reflect in choral ode the sympathy that Neoptolemus cannot help feeling for the cripple. When they re-emerge from the cave, Neoptolemus is given another opportunity to make off with the bow. Philoctetes, overcome with a spasm of pain, gives the bow to the young man to look after in case some-one steals it, and promptly faints. When he comes round Neoptolemus refuses to give it back and confesses the truth. Basically an honest man, Neoptolemus' conscience is by this time in such a muddle that Philoctetes has almost persuaded him to hand the bow back when Odysseus returns. In the scene which follows Neoptolemus is holding the bow, but the argument involves only Philoctetes and Odysseus. So the action proceeds with the Chorus, as sailors of Neoptolemus, serving throughout to amplify his changing loyalties while the bow itself dictates the visual action and dominates the stage sequence.

This special emphasis on a single prop is paralleled at a different level in the play by another variation on the tri-angular scene. The novelty of the first confrontation between Odysseus, Neoptolemus and Philoctetes resides in Odysseus' disguise as a merchant. The first part of the scene has Odysseus talking to Neoptolemus and pretending not to see Philoctetes, though he makes sure he is speaking loudly enough to be over-heard. The scene is echoed later in the play when Neoptolemus has suffered a change of heart. Philoctetes has discovered the truth and Odysseus appears in his own person. The real issues of the play are only seen to emerge once all pretence has been dropped. Neoptolemus is finally convinced that his promise to

---

2 *Greek Tragedy in Action*, London, Methuen, 1978, p. 90.

see Philoctetes safely home is more important than his obligations to the Greeks at Troy.

At this juncture with Odysseus put to flight and the play
apparently moving towards the wrong conclusion, wrong for
the myth that is, not for personal morality, Heracles arrives *ex
machina* and persuades the characters that it must be otherwise. Heracles, the original owner of the bow, appears as a god
above the mortals to direct the course of the future. The bow
which has been the focus of the stage action is elevated to the
level of divine aid. Philoctetes subordinates his private will to
the community at large and finally submits to Fate.

Oedipus Tyrannus has all the ambiguity of the great play. No
interpretation can be definitive, no production entirely satis-
fying. It holds a unique position in the world's literature, but
this must not be allowed to take precedence over its theatrical
merits.

As in the case of Philoctetes, the 'fate' of Oedipus is defined
in strengths and weaknesses. Oedipus, the tyrant of Thebes, is
doomed even before the play starts, by a combination of factors,
principal among them his own nature. Though Apollo has
twice given warnings, first to Laius that his son will kill him,
later to Oedipus that he will marry his mother and kill his
father, human weakness betrays the characters when both
Jocasta and Oedipus believe they can avoid what Fate has
decreed, or, if you prefer, the future of which Apollo has
foreknowledge.

Oedipus is drawn as a man of contrasting qualities, all of
which are pinpointed in the title of the play, so inadequately
translated as *Oedipus the King* or *Oedipus Rex*. The Greek term
turannos is both neutral and material. Literally it means no
more than an unconstitutional ruler, but to an Athenian ear it
still smacked of the latter days of the Pisistratid family driven
out in 510 BC. Oedipus, for all his temporal power is shared with
Jocasta and Creon, makes the decisions. When the state is in
trouble, the citizens appeal to Oedipus as their *turannos*, a
forceful but benign *turannos* whose concern for his people is
never in doubt. When it is suggested, however, that there is a
curse on Thebes, the Chorus are able to give the term a rather
different meaning. '*Hubris* engenders the *turannos*', they sing,
and when it becomes a choice between loyalty to god or man,
they are quite clear where their allegiances must lie. Ironically

Oedipus is not a *turannos* at all. He is the legitimate son of the previous king. But he does possess the qualities of a *turannos* for both good and ill. He is impetuous and forceful, but suspicious and curiously narrow in vision.

The argument that the *Oedipus Tyrannus* is an extensive image of Athens under the leadership of Pericles is strong enough to support the provisional dating of 429 BC, just before Pericles' death. In the early years of the Peloponnesian war when the city was crowded with farmers and metics seeking security from the ravages of the Spartan army, plague broke out. Though Pericles was himself to fall victim, he was seen in many quarters to be responsible not only for promoting the war but for compounding the attendant discomfort.

Oedipus Tyrannus opens with the picture of a city struck by plague. Oedipus enters and addresses the citizens:

> My children, youngest offspring of ancient Cadmus, why do you cluster round these shrines, wreathed in suppliant olive-branches? (1–3)

There is little likelihood that Oedipus was meant to address the audience here. The actions he refers to are specific. Though some commentators prefer to believe that a crowd of citizens entered for this scene only and left again before the arrival of the Chorus, by far the most satisfactory interpretation of the stage-craft is to assume that the Chorus made their entry as the citizens of Thebes appealing for help. This first entrance, however produced, must surely have presented a powerful picture to the audience. In the production by Karolos Koun for the 1969 World Theatre Season in London, even on the proscenium-arch stage of the Aldwych Theatre, that first choral entry took over six minutes. The haunting image of a city in mourning was powerful enough to permeate the entire production. What made it so forceful was that the entrance took place in complete silence. It is certainly unusual for a chorus to enter in silence, but then silence is as much a part of the theatre language of Sophocles as of any other classical playwright.

By the opening of the play Oedipus has come to represent the only hope of salvation. In succeeding scenes the Chorus find their confidence in him whittled away as his own position is steadily undermined by the revelations of the past. That such a reversal can and indeed must be physically reinforced in performance should be self-evident and, as one would expect, Sophocles promotes it in a number of striking effects.

The triangular scene is used on three occasions. On the first a violent quarrel between Creon and Oedipus is broken up by Jocasta, sister to one, wife and mother to the other.

The second occasion incorporates the most telling visual moment in the play. When the Messenger arrives from Corinth and tells Oedipus that his supposed parents are dead, Oedipus reacts by informing him of the oracle he received which kept him from returning home to Corinth. To allay his fears the Messenger then tells him that he was not the child of the King of Corinth but a foundling discovered exposed on Mount Cithaeron. All this is revealed in dialogue of almost painful deliberation. The most important character in the scene never interrupts the *stichomuthia*, but at some time during the discussion which eases the fears of both Oedipus and the Messenger, Jocasta realizes the full truth. It is she, not Oedipus or the Messenger, who needs to be the centre of attention. The play reaches its climax in her realization, and as the two men turn to her, she can only warn Oedipus to proceed no further before retiring indoors to kill herself.

Sophocles follows this up with a further three-handed scene in which the Shepherd who first exposed Oedipus as a child is forced to reveal the truth so plainly that even Oedipus can understand it. The tension of this scene is dependent on the parallel to the previous one in which Oedipus' confidence is revived, only to be shattered as the whole truth is told and the Messenger comes to realize his own involvement.

The play's central image is again a visual one, initially demonstrated by the arrival of Teiresias, the blind seer, a regular visitor to the tragic stage. The immediate physical contrast between Teiresias and Oedipus is an obvious one but no less striking for that. Teiresias is old, Oedipus young; Teiresias is led by a child, Oedipus puts all his trust in himself; Teiresias is physically blind with inner vision, Oedipus believes his intelligence supreme because he was the one to defeat the Sphinx.

When Oedipus finally discovers the truth about himself, he puts out his eyes. Only when physically blind does he acquire full understanding. Sophocles' staging of the scene in which he returns from blinding himself clearly stresses the contrasts. It may well be that the actor playing Oedipus changed his mask before this last entrance, but in a theatre it is not the eyes which give him away. An audience tells that a man is blind not by his eyes but by his hands. Oedipus, the confident leader who prides himself on his forcefulness and foresight, returns from the palace unable even to tell where he is. Teiresias had his boy to lead him, his staff to support him. Oedipus has nothing. His children are brought before him and he can only feel for them. At the last he is utterly dependent on other people. The reversal is total.

Though separated by so many years in the writing, *Oedipus at Colonus* always seems to pick up exactly where *Oedipus Tyrannus* leaves off. The play opens with the blind man led on by his daughter Antigone, now grown up. Oedipus too is older, so much so that he becomes aware that this is to be his final resting-place. They have reached Colonus, just outside Athens, and the set represents a grove, sacred to the Furies. Despite Oedipus' intuition about the place, a passer-by warns him that he must not rest there and runs off to seek help when Oedipus asks for sanctuary. The peace of the grove is soon shattered by the arrival of the Chorus:

> Look. Who was it? Where is he now? Where can he be this foreigner, this most outrageous man? Look about, search him out. Leave no stone unturned. (118–23)

This clamorous entrance, a far cry from the measured tread envisaged by later critics, serves to stress Oedipus' isolation, deprived of human contact because of his past. The Chorus order him out of the grove and indicate where he may sit, but their concern at this time is over the violation of the grove. When Oedipus reveals who he is, they are fearful that he will pollute them simply by being there, but agree to refer the matter to Theseus.

It is at this juncture that Ismene arrives with the news that, old and feeble as he is, Oedipus has some use, or at least his dead body will have, and Thebes wants him back. An oracle has revealed that the country in which his bones are finally laid to rest will benefit and Creon intends to take no chances. When Theseus offers friendship and a refuge, Oedipus gratefully accepts, only to be confronted by Creon who has kidnapped Ismene and now intends to carry off Antigone and Oedipus too. Here, as elsewhere, Oedipus' utter helplessness is emphasized:

ANTIGONE: Friends, friends, I am being dragged away.
OEDIPUS: My child, where are you?
ANTIGONE: Forced away.
OEDIPUS: Stretch out your hands.
ANTIGONE: I cannot.
CREON: Take her away.
OEDIPUS: Ah, how helpless I am.
CREON: You can no more lean on these two crutches. (843–9)

Despite the intervention of the Chorus, Creon tries to drag Oedipus away too, to be thwarted only by the return of Theseus who saves Oedipus and restores his daughters to him. The subsequent arrival of Oedipus' son Polyneices exaggerates the episodic nature of the play, but reinforces the point that, except in Athens, people are only interested in Oedipus for what they can get out of him.

There are several striking similarities to the final work of a number of later playwrights, Shakespeare and Ibsen among them. The old man's search for peace of mind, as well as rest for his bones, has a personal ring to it. It is not, I would think, too fanciful to connect the story of Sophocles' son attempting to have him declared legally senile with the furious outburst with which Oedipus dismisses Polyneices.

But the play is not to end in bitterness and, after the departure of Polyneices, Sophocles achieves a transformation. Not perhaps as startling and comprehensive as the scene with which Aeschylus brings the *Oresteia* to its conclusion, the transfiguration of Oedipus has a peculiar beauty. As thunder booms out and lightning flashes (as the scene is described by the Chorus), Oedipus recognizes a signal that the end of his life is close. In a thrilling moment whose theatrical force depends entirely on the audience having witnessed his frailty for the first fifteen hundred lines, Oedipus utters the following words:

Now, children, follow me. Wonderfully, I will be your leader, just as for so long you were mine. Come, but do not touch me. Let me find the sacred tomb where I am destined to lie hidden. This way, this way. This way Hermes leads me, guide of the dead. (1543–8)

With firm step and steady vision, the old stooped figure of the early play leads his daughters and the King along and out the *parodos*. No moment in Greek drama more strongly suggests faith in a divine purpose. Reasonably the Chorus presume he is going to his death:

> O child of Earth and Tartarus, I beseech you to escort him in safety to the abode of the dead. (1573–6)

Such is their prayer, but the Messenger who reports what has happened reveals something more mystical. After bidding his children goodbye, Oedipus was summoned by a voice. The Messenger and the girls turned away. When they looked back, Oedipus had vanished. Antigone and Ismene return to sing a lament for their father, tinged with relief that he has finally found rest. The play ends in a mood of exaltation and wonder at what was has taken place.

Where Aeschylus paints in large strokes and sudden moments of telling impact, Sophocles uses his dramatic technique to engage sympathy for the individual. There is a sense of realism here, but 'realism' is a comparative term. The realism of Sophocles cannot easily be compared with the sardonic modernity of Euripides to whom we must now turn.

7

EURIPIDES:
THE TRAGEDIES

Euripides has left nineteen plays to posterity. It may be fortuitous that so many have survived compared to the much smaller
number of Aeschylus and Sophocles, but there is not one which
fails to exemplify his dramatic method. In simple terms,
Euripides uses surprise. Sometimes the effect is shocking,
sometimes humorous. Occasionally the text that has been
handed down is so baffling as to require emendation, even if
there is no external evidence of later tampering. So much of this
adjusting of plays seems to have taken place before Lycurgus
introduced his law in the late fourth century BC to standardize
texts that the critic has to be tentative in the extreme in how he
interprets or explains Euripides' purpose. When, for example,
in *Orestes* Menelaus is arguing with Orestes, who stands on the
roof of the palace with a sword at Hermione's throat, he appeals
to Pylades, Orestes's companion, 'You, Pylades, are you his
accomplice in this murder?' But it is Orestes who replies, 'He
says so, though silent. Let my speaking suffice'.

What are we to make of such a speech at such a time? Does
the dialogue suggest that Pylades is reluctant to be involved?
Might Menelaus be intent on distracting Orestes in order to
save his daughter's life? Or is Orestes covering up for Pylades'
inability to speak because he is being played by an 'extra' at this
point, only three actors being available and the third about to
appear as Apollo?

There are pitfalls of all kinds in assessing such a scene and to suggest a final answer would be rash. What one can say with confidence is that the stage picture presented at this moment is unusual and potent. Menelaus and his soldiers have been beating at the locked door below. Orestes and Pylades are on the roof with Hermione as hostage. They are brandishing flaming torches with which they threaten to burn down the palace. And at any moment Apollo will arrive with the dead body of Menelaus' wife Helen to sort out all their troubles by telling Orestes not to slit Hermione's throat, but to marry her instead.

The most immediate difference between Euripides and the earlier playwrights is in the dramatic language he uses. Consider the following passage from *Madness of Heracles* where Lycus addresses Amphitryon and Megara, the father and wife of Heracles:

> How far you parade your grief beyond what's decent, because you have to die; one who filled Greece with hollow boast of how Zeus was co-father of your son; the other so proud to be called wife of the noblest man alive. What was so marvellous in what Heracles did? The fact he killed a hydra in a bog? Or the lion of Nemea? He trapped it in a snare, and only says he strangled it with bare hands. (146–52)

Or Orestes to his sister in *Iphigeneia in Tauris*:

> Even the gods, for all they are called wise, are no more to be trusted than fleeting dreams. Amongst the gods, no less than mortal men, confusion reigns. (570–3)

Or again Hermione to Andromache in *Andromache*:

> Such a pitch of brazenness you reached, you bitch, you slept with the man who killed your husband, and bore the murderer's children. Foreigners, they're all alike. Father in bed with daughter, mother with son. Sister and brother at it. The closest make progress by slaughter, and no law to stop them. (170–7)

To which the incensed Andromache replies in kind:

> It needed no drugs of mine to turn your husband off you. The fact you're unfit to live with was enough. . . . O Hector, so dear to me. Even when Aphrodite led you astray, I accepted

your latest love, acted wet-nurse to your love-children even, to save you from bitterness. And acted so, as a wife should, in duty to her husband. But you are so jealous over your man, you daren't let him out in the wet. When it comes to having it off with men, don't try to compete with Helen. The wise child avoids the mother's vice. (205–6; 222–31)

Whatever later additions there may have been to Euripides' plays, we must assume that the majority of such speeches, and there are any number of examples to choose from, were written by Euripides and could not have been written by Aeschylus or Sophocles. When the invective is so splenetic, the disillusion so harsh, it can be no surprise that Euripides should have suffered more than most playwrights from the accusation of approving the sentiments of his characters. Where Sophocles could present the arguments of Antigone, Ismene and Creon as the unavoidable clash of irreconcilable opposites, Euripides creates arguers dominated by despair, or by spite, or by any one of a variety of poisoned and personal passions. Some of Euripides' characters sound like politicians and lawyers, others like hysterical witnesses, but they speak in the tones of the time in which Euripides lived. The *Oresteia* may be taken to provide the playwright's comment on the relationship of justice to contemporary democracy, but the setting is in prehistory. In *Orestes* Euripides has his protagonists criticized for failing to resort to a legal system which is not far removed from that of the Athens in which he is writing.

In this way Euripides builds up an ethos which, if it does not unveil his own attitudes, can at least be seen to reflect the anxious war-torn years of the late fifth century BC. There is clearly some danger in looking for the man even in the mood of his pieces, but Euripides was no Seneca, sitting solemnly in his study creating closet dramas according to moralistic formulae. The picture Aristophanes creates of him, for all the artistic licence of the comic dramatist, must be one that the audiences of Athens would have recognized. It may even be that Euripides wrote from life in a Strindbergian sense and that the Helens of his plays, which vary from the slightly scatty to the decidedly flighty, reflect his own reputedly unfortunate relationships with women. That is the kind of writer Euripides was. His work encourages speculation on the man. If Aristophanes is any guide, the Athenians of his time were similarly intrigued.

Euripides' particular talent as a playwright resides in the locating of complex and realistic emotions and responses in plays presented under precisely the same physical conditions as were most of Sophocles'. 'New wine in old bottles' was how the nineteenth-century scholar William Merry described the method, but it is rather more than that. You need to make an imaginative leap of a high order to appreciate how the sentiments of Euripides' characters might have sounded to an audience encountering them for the first time at a festival whose prime purpose was to ally religious observance to civic ceremonial. Patriotic sentiments, once applauded by the whole house, may make us smile at the remove of 2400 years, though less so perhaps than similar sentiments in our own theatre of less than a hundred years ago. But how are we to remind ourselves that Medea, Phaedra and Andromache were all male actors in masks? Yet this is how Euripides paints his picture. The theatre is the theatre of Sophocles, the sentiments forensic, philosophic, domestic.

Far from being disadvantaged by the stage conditions of his time, Euripides married the visual to the aural, quite deliberately. In no way was he hampered by the paradox this sometimes posed, as his detractors, and even some of his apologists, would have us believe. He set out purposefully to concentrate the mind in a manner that today we might loosely call Brechtian. This may even be part of the reason for his emphasizing female characters to such an extent that fourteen of the eighteen tragic choruses (the nineteenth play is a satyr play) are composed of women, while eight of these have an eponymous heroine.

In Euripides, then, we should look for a theatrical sense rooted less in the thematic image than in the sudden reversal, as much a novelty to the audience as to the characters themselves. Most of the plays offer examples of the technique, and if 'reversal' and 'recognition', *peripeteia* and *anagnorisis*, are weapons that Aristotle understood to be constituents of any tragedy, there is always something individual about a Euripides treatment. Many more plays of Euripides survive than of Aeschylus and Sophocles together and it would be tedious in the present context to consider each in turn. Five of them I will examine in the next chapter as comedies, though they are not comedies by any classical definition. One, *Cyclops*, is the only complete satyr play to survive; *Alcestis* was presented last in a group submission, but is neither satyric nor tragic; *Iphigeneia in Tauris*, *Helen* and *Ion* were generically tragedies, but look forward in atmosphere to the new comedy of the fourth century and beyond.

Five more, *Medea*, *Madness of Heracles*, *Trojan Women*, *Electra* and *Bacchae* show a positive development in stage technique. They too merit individual attention.

Rather than ignore the remaining nine, which would give a largely specious order of preference to the others, I will consider them as a group, but only in order to point out some of their common features. What a conspectus view of Euripides reveals is the playwright's sheer delight in the process of theatre. Aeschylus and Sophocles may have shared it but only for Euripides did its exploration become almost an end in itself.

Suppliants poses a specific problem related to the Chorus which threatens to undermine any attempt to use the texts of Greek plays to interpret the action. The play is a fairly jingoistic piece, perhaps inspired by some incident in the Peloponnesian War. The main issue is the fate of the bodies of the seven heroes killed in the attack on Thebes, which Aeschylus dramatized in his *Seven Against Thebes*. The Chorus are the mothers of the seven and the problem is simply that there are not enough of them. Aethra, in the prologue, talks of them as seven, even though one of the heroes was Polyneices, whose mother is Jocasta. Jocasta does figure in the play, but not as one of the Chorus. That leaves six, which with attendants could make a nice round twelve. But twelve is the number commonly believed to have formed the chorus only in Aeschylus, and raised by Sophocles to fifteen.

A complication is added when the bodies of the slain are introduced. Not only is Polyneices patently not among them, but neither it would appear, is Amphiareus, son of Oicles, who had the good luck to be carried off by the gods while still alive. The mothers who ought by this time to be only six, if not five, listen to the eulogy for the slain and sing a dirge, 'Seven mothers who gave birth to seven sons'. The bodies are cremated together, except for that of Capaneus, onto whose pyre his widow Evadne leaps from the palace roof. Another of the 'seven' mothers is also the mother of Evadne, but she makes no prescribed reaction as an individual to the extraordinary suicide. The ashes are then brought back on stage by the sons of the slain, of whom logically there should be only five. But by this time the would-be director is in a state of near panic.

In Aeschylus' play *Suppliants* (on a different theme entirely) it is generally assumed that a chorus of twelve served to represent the fifty daughters of Danaus. That seems perfectly in keeping with a drama which makes the most perfunctory of gestures towards realism. It is quite a different matter to have a chorus, and in a Euripides play at that, announcing that they are seven mothers of seven dead heroes, when as mothers they ought to be less than seven and as a chorus they ought to be more.

Nor is there any satisfactory solution to the problem, though many have been promoted over the years. We seem to be faced either with an aberration caused by a fourth-century revival text, or a precedent for divorcing the spoken word entirely from theatrical presentation. It would appear that for this play at any rate, the Chorus are a group who do not function as the individuals they say they are. The central picture of the sorrowing mothers and sons contrasted to all the political talk of the inevitability of war is still a powerful comment, but the actual staging of the text as it stands presents a problem amenable to solution only by assuming that the Chorus take on the total role of 'motherhood'. It is a salutary warning against confusing literal and figurative levels in the interpretation of even a late Greek stage text.

Orestes has a great deal of action, some of it blatantly comic, but the overall mood is savage. The heroine of *Electra* is here a more pragmatic figure, devoted to a brother who is at the outset deranged, not, as she points out, because of the Furies but from conscience. For this play is set in Argos in the aftermath of the murder of Clytemnestra, with Orestes and Electra receiving scant sympathy for their deed. This is an Argos with a legal system quite capable of coping with any family dispute, even such a one as that to which the house of Atreus is heir. The Argive assembly is intent on having Orestes and Electra stoned to death. How they escape from this fate is the substance of the plot, but in the process the pair of them, and Pylades too, are revealed as more ruthless and barbaric than their mother ever was. To escape the fate decreed for them, Pylades and Orestes first murder Helen while Electra eggs them on: 'Kill, butcher, destroy her. Guide your twin swords, thrusting them into her'. Then they capture Helen's daughter, Hermione: 'Hold her, hold her. And shut her up, sword at her throat'. Greek tragedy may only rarely show scenes of violence, but Euripides creates here characters who live by and for nothing else. And yet the play is lightened by a comic Messenger speaking in pidgin Greek and the entry of a Chorus whose lines seem calculated to draw attention to the incongruity of their presence. Both these incidents will illustrate in the next chapter Euripides' feeling for the comic.

There may be fourth-century amendments within the received text of *Orestes*. There are certainly difficulties with the texts of several other plays and care needs to be taken before fathering on Euripides a theatrical technique to which he himself would have laid no claims. *Iphigeneia in Aulis* is a case in point. The story of how Agamemnon tricked Clytemnestra into bringing their daughter to Aulis on the pretext of marrying Achilles, but in reality so that he could offer her as a human sacrifice, contains an ending that scholars almost unanimously reject as spurious. The reason that they dislike it is that it lets the tragedy off the hook. A Messenger arrives to proclaim that at the very last moment Iphigeneia was translated and a hind substituted. Though such an ending prevents the play from becoming particularly moving, it does serve to illuminate and emphasize the positive aspects of a story which in its plot alone appears inordinately cruel. Euripides' starting point is myth which handed down that Agamemnon had his daughter sacrificed. As ever he looks for a new dimension in the story and, with the aid of a variant version, changes the emphasis. As we will see later he has already approached the story of Helen in much the same way.

In the *Iphigeneia in Aulis* we are again looking at a family. There is more physical contact between characters than in perhaps any other tragedy and usually it is a friendly contact. Menelaus does wrestle with the Old Man over a letter which he is carrying on behalf of Agamemnon, but the brothers soon clasp hands in reconciliation. Iphigeneia, when she arrives, turns out to be a devoted daughter who embraces her father with real affection and is upset by his rejection of her. She and her mother Clytemnestra have brought the baby Orestes with them. He is treated both as an integral part of Agamemnon's family and as a reminder to the audience of the future course of the family fortunes. Clytemnestra requires physical help to get down from the chariot in which she arrives, and then Achilles, who has no knowledge of the trick marriage, finds Clytemnestra clasping him by the hand as her future son-in-law. The climax of the story reinforces this. Iphigeneia accepts that she is to be sacrificed. She takes the baby Orestes and embraces him, but when her mother volunteers to accompany her, Iphigeneia rejects the offer. These actions, referred to within the text itself, reveal a pattern of behaviour as full of small affections and honourable generosity as the story can permit. An ending which preserves Iphigeneia from slaughter, and purports to show a reconciliation between Agamemnon and Clytemnestra may ring a little hollow, but it is at least of a part with the playwright's main approach.

Iphigeneia in Aulis is one of a small number of plays which open at night. *Electra* is another, but almost the entire action of *Rhesus* is meant to take place under the cover of darkness. Darkness indeed becomes in itself an element of the Euripidean in-joke, homage to the fact that the theatre is, after all, only the theatre. *Rhesus* is a perplexing play which has variously been described as early, late or spurious on a variety of textual and linguistic grounds, these being the standard critical means of accommodating awkward material. It is the only surviving play which deals with an incident from the *Iliad*, but much of it is unorthodox. There is a Chorus of sentries who function as sentries first and Chorus second. They leave the stage when their replacements fail to turn up, but return in time to capture Odysseus and Diomedes who have sneaked into the Trojan camp, then let them get away because Odysseus knows the password and claims to have seen some intruders. Even a modern production witnessed at night in the theatre at Delphi could not prevent the proceedings from appearing faintly ludicrous, the more so because the scene in which the Chorus are absent is dominated by the goddess Athene fooling Odysseus by pretending to be Aphrodite.

The point is, of course, that, as in the classic of Pekin Opera and Peter Shaffer's *Black Comedy*, all of these confusions are attributable to the dark. Whether the entire action was presented as though the characters could not see one another, or whether the Chorus carried torches, or any other convention was

employed, is unresolvable. *Rhesus* is, like *Orestes*, a play of
action and event, and if it seems to lack the flare of the best of
Euripides, it does explore further the contrast between outward
and inward appearances which so dominates Euripidean stage
technique.

Andromache is another play which presents problems to the
commentators, this time because of a later story that it was not
performed in Athens, at least when it was first written. Here the
visual contrasts are again principally linked to the vicissitudes
of fortune. Andromache, the former wife of Hector, is now
married to Neoptolemus, to whom she was allotted after the
sack of Troy. That security is now threatened because Neoptolemus has married Hermione who wants the 'slave-wife' killed.
Andromache and her son are saved by Peleus and it is Hermione
who finds herself in danger. Out of the blue, Orestes arrives and
goes off to kill Neoptolemus. Eventually Thetis arrives *ex
machina* to tell Andromache to marry Helenus in Molossia. All
these abrupt reversals have some physical reinforcement with
Andromache and her son tied together until they are rescued
and the distraught Hermione tearing her hair in frustration, but
the main interest of the play resides in the splendidly spiteful
encounters between the central characters, some of which I
recorded earlier.

Hecuba presents changes from weakness to strength more
akin to those of *Trojan Women*, but with some features to give
it individuality. The play opens with a prologue from the ghost
of Polydorus, Hecuba's last remaining son, of whose death she
is not made aware until much later. This ghost, as one image
of futility, is paralleled by the ghost of Achilles to which
Hecuba's daughter Polyxena is to be sacrificed, though this
second ghost has no direct part in the action. The effect is
rounded off when a corpse is returned under a sheet after
Polyxena has been taken away for sacrifice and the mother
removes it to discover the body, not of her daughter to whose
death she has steeled herself, but of her son whom she, as
opposed to the audience, still believes living.

Hecuba herself is possessed of a rare strength. Reduced
though she is, the former queen of Troy resolves on revenge
against Polymestor, her son's murderer. Lulled into a false
sense of security Polymestor enters her tent with his young
sons. They are set upon by Hecuba's women, the boys murdered,

the father blinded. Hecuba's first entrance in the play is on all fours, as the ghost of her son attests. Now it is Polymestor who crawls on, 'Must I follow the step of a four-footed mountain-beast, placing foot after hand?' Hecuba stands by remorseless as Polymestor serves as the Messenger of his own fate as well as a *deus* to forecast the future for Hecuba and Agamemnon.

Phoenician Women also has the climactic entrance of a blind man, but this in a play set against the Theban civil war, and the blind man is Oedipus. The play opens with Jocasta, immediately advertising how different this is to be from the Sophoclean classic. Now, some time after the events which form the *Oedipus Tyrannus*, Oedipus still lives in Thebes, but has been locked up by his sons. Despite the agreement to rule year and year about, Eteocles intends to remain in office. After the scene has been set by Jocasta, there is a sequence similar to the opening of *Troilus and Cressida* when Antigone is taken up to the roof of the palace, apparently by means of a visible staircase from stage floor to roof, to review the opposing forces.

The civil war which afflicts the whole city is depicted very much in family terms, with Jocasta and her children, Antigone, Polyneices and Eteocles, her brother Creon and his son Menoecus all featured in the action. Even the Chorus, who give the play its title, are distant relations, though, not being from Thebes, they are in a position to give a dispassionate if not disinterested assessment. Eteocles and Polyneices kill each other and Jocasta commits suicide, all the bodies being brought back to the stage. Then and only then does Oedipus make his entrance, forced to listen to Antigone arguing with Creon. In a moving final scene the blind man feels the faces of his dead wife and his sons laid out, one upon the other. In *Seven Against Thebes* Aeschylus had avoided a stage confrontation between the warring brothers. In *Phoenician Women* Euripides shows it, but he does not always include the expected scene.

In *Hippolytus* the name character never meets his step-mother Phaedra, whose passion for him leads her to suicide, leaving a note accusing him of rape. The play is framed by the rival goddesses Aphrodite and Artemis, the one forecasting the action of the play while professing her hatred for Hippolytus, the other revealing herself at the end to convince Theseus of his son's innocence. The play proper begins unusually, with a hunting chorus who would be more at home in the world of

Viennese operetta than Greek tragedy. No sooner have they
retired than the main chorus arrive, a group of local women. For
the ensuing third of the play not a single male character is
involved. The play passes through extremes of mood between
Hippolytus' entrance with the huntsmen and his on-stage
death, but they are no more than an extension of the tragic
reversal from prosperity to disaster. As in other plays this is
amplified by physical contrasts, usually in the form of strength
or weakness. Hippolytus is first seen in all his splendour as a
hunter, complete with attendants and the paraphernalia of the
hunt, in order to make the contrast with the broken figure
brought back to die. This is balanced by the visual parallel
between the dying Hippolytus and the fading Phaedra, whose
first entrance is made wheeled in on a couch.

Children of Heracles carries such physical contrasts to their
extreme. If there is a single theme to the play, it must be the
helplessness of childhood and old age in the face of brute
force – though in this case the bullies get their come-uppance.
The plot is full of improbable heroics and is far too complicated
to summarize. It is packed with references to the fact that you
can only expect to find justice among Athenians and is even set
at Marathon, the site of the most famous of all Athenian mili-
tary triumphs.

The visual effect of the play is concentrated in the character
of Iolaus, an old man of considerable decrepitude, who is
attempting to protect the children of Heracles, after the death of
their father, from the tyrant Eurystheus. Iolaus is easily thrown
to the ground by Copreus, Eurystheus' herald, but when it
comes to a battle, Iolaus is determined to take part, despite the
scorn of an attendant who has the job of dressing him in his
armour on stage. Their nineteen-line exit, 'Do you see how I
hurry along?' 'I can see how you think you are hurrying', is by
far the longest in Greek drama and formidably comic. Even
more incongruous is the transformation which a Messenger
reports, though he has not seen it himself, as taking place on the
battlefield when Iolaus 'regains his youth' and captures
Eurystheus. The audience are not given the opportunity to see
the old man in his rejuvenation, but as the play reaches its
conclusion and Eurystheus is unceremoniously condemned to
death, Iolaus' stubborn valour remains.

All the above plays have original features and some of them

are among the tragedies most worthy of revival. Five of the more tragic, however, manage to capture between them the individuality of Euripides and his special contribution to theatrical technique.

The first of the five tragedies I have singled out is *Medea*. *Medea* is firmly dated to 431 BC, before the Peloponnesian War and when Pericles was still alive. More significantly this means that it was produced before Sophocles' *Oedipus Tyrannus* or *Women of Trachis*. The setting of the play presents no problem, the *skene* representing a house with a single door, sufficient, with the two *parodoi*, for the various entrances and exits of the seven speaking characters.

Again, unexceptionally, the play opens with the entrance of a minor character, Medea's nurse, to deliver a prologue to the audience. As a part of his dramatic method Euripides often makes use of the frame plot, which allows a character to set the scene at the beginning and establish the myth, or that aspect of it which the playwright intends to treat. The play then unfolds with plot developing according to the motivation of the individuals concerned, often to a point at which the myth can only be rescued by divine intervention. This was less a retreat on the part of the playwright than a means of liberating a received plot. The myth frames the play proper. Between, the human beings take over.

In *Medea* Euripides contrives to set up an expected *dénouement*, then purposely surprises the audience by a visual trick which depends on their familiarity with the manner in which plays normally come to a conclusion. The prologue helps to set up the surprise. The Nurse begins by rehearsing the story of Jason who stole the golden fleece from Colchis thanks to the help of Medea, the king's daughter. She committed murder to save him, and since her return with him to Corinth, has borne him two children. Now, several years later, Jason is abandoning her to marry the king of Corinth's daughter.

As the prologue ends, the play proper opens with the arrival along the *parodos* of the two children of Jason and Medea, escorted by their tutor. Almost half of Euripides' surviving plays feature children, usually in a parlous state because of the viciousness of their elders. This, of course, is the principal reason for introducing them, in that it contrasts the innocence of childhood with the corruption of maturity. The parallel to

Athenian lawcourt practice in pleading a defendant's case
is an obvious one, when the possible plight of the children
was exploited as a prime means of swaying a jury unimpressed
by mere argument. These children were clearly played by
child actors (whether or not in small masks is a matter of
speculation), and what to a twentieth-century audience might
appear little more than a sentimental gesture, perhaps a cynical
one, was to the Athenians of the classical period well in
keeping with a judicial process at once advanced and rather
dubious.

The children in *Medea* do not speak on-stage, but have a vital
role within the drama. Because they appear at the beginning,
they become easily fixed in the audience's mind both as the
embodiment of Medea's love for Jason and the instruments
of his downfall when that love becomes warped. They listen as
the Nurse and the Tutor talk of exile, and the Nurse turns to
them:

Do you hear, children what sort of man your father is to you?
Would he were dead. No, he is my master, though he has
treated his dear ones shamefully. (82–4)

The Nurse then warns the Tutor to take the children indoors
and keep them away from their mother, but before they can
leave, Medea is heard off-stage, wishing that she might die. The
Tutor hurries the children away, but they stay in the mind as
the pivot for the tragic action. Later they return with their
mother to bid farewell to a Jason who believes he has effected a
reconciliation with Medea. The scene's chilling quality resides
in the audience's prior knowledge that she has already resolved
to kill them. Before they meet their own fate, Medea makes
them instruments in the first part of her revenge. They carry a
poisoned dress and crown as wedding presents from her for
Jason's new wife. A choral ode later they return, having delivered the fatal gifts, with news of a reprieve from exile. Medea
takes her leave of them: 'Why do you stare at me children, why
smile so your last ever smile?' (1010–1). Her resolve almost
breaks, but not quite, and the audience sees not the villainess
who callously will murder her children, but a woman so driven
to desperation by Jason that she will kill them as the only
means of damaging him as he has damaged her.

The other conflicts in the play are powerful but predictable. Ironies are compounded by deceipt, by the false gifts and by the curious position in which the Chorus find themselves, partly appalled by what is happening, but sufficiently sympathetic not to interfere. They sing constantly of the children but decline to be involved, even when Euripides goes so far as to have the children call for help as Medea pursues them to their death. Jason arrives to be informed of the murders and the Chorus bid him open the doors to witness the dreadful sight.

What the audience is expecting at this juncture is the presentation of a tableau on the *ekkuklema*, wheeled out from behind the central entrance. This is what happens in every similar scene in the surviving plays. Instead, the focus of attention is diverted upwards to the roof of the palace above the doors. There Medea appears apparently in a chariot, provided by her grandfather Helios, the Sun, to defend her from her enemies. By a remarkable stroke Medea becomes her own *dea ex machina*. At first glance, she gets away with what she has done, but by this time we are witnessing the concluding part of the frame and a different Medea permits a return to the received myth which guarantees her escape. A touch of reality remains as she justifies her actions, but she is now beyond pain. Literally, as the audience see it, she stands above what she has done, while Jason is left below vainly striving to touch the dead bodies of the children which he is simply unable to reach. The drop curtain of a modern theatre would seal the tableau and confirm it. As it is, with no real way of knowing how the characters might have got off the stage, the action is incomplete. The basis of it is clear enough, however. Alive or dead, it is the children who unite the play and whose presence reveals a stagecraft to make of the *Medea* something both deeper and more immediate than a mere story of vicious revenge.

Euripides uses children in *Madness of Heracles* as well. The hero's small sons, together with their mother Megara and grandfather Amphitryon, open the play as suppliants. These children have been condemned to death by Lycus, pretender to the throne of Thebes, in Heracles' absence. They are reprieved when their father arrives home, only to succumb to a fit of madness which seizes him. Variations to the Heracles legend were legion, and it posed no obvious problem to an Athenian audience to encounter a Heracles play in which the hero slaughters his children, only a few years after Euripides had presented a *Children of Heracles* and perhaps also close in time to the production of Sophocles' *Women of Trachis*, which offers yet another version of Heracles' fate.

Still less was a Greek audience concerned that a character should present utterly different characteristics in different plays. The Heracles of *Alcestis* is a mixture of drunken buffoon and heroic saviour, while in *Madness of Heracles*, Euripides creates a powerful man, victim both of his reputation and of the fickleness of the gods. The play presents another series of contrasts between strength and weakness, as we have seen in several plays of both Euripides and Sophocles. But in *Madness of Heracles* the sense of paradox is given an added dimension by being set against the difference between prosperity and destitution and the apparently arbitrary factors which create the gap. The first part of the plot shows how this works.

Amphitryon introduces Megara and her three children in a prologue. As a suppliant group they were perhaps wheeled on, Amphitryon detaching himself from them to tell the audience their story. Heracles is believed dead because he has not returned after visiting Hades to bring back the three-headed dog Cerberus, the last of his twelve labours. Lycus has taken over and intends to kill Megara and the children to confirm his position. Megara stresses her own fall and the isolation of her position. The Chorus do not appear to offer much help, 'leaning on sticks. . .no more than a voice. . .a walking dream. . . tremulous'.

Though they exhibit rather more energy in later choral passages, they are about as feeble as any chorus can be. Lycus, on the other hand, is bursting with health, so much so that in his first speech he can debunk Heracles' feats of strength. This demolition of the past is put in perspective by a hundred-line chorus in celebration of Heracles' exploits and, from a position that appears hopeless, the fortunes of Heracles' family start to revive.

Megara and the children get dressed in the 'garments of the grave', apparently reconciled to death, only for Heracles to arrive in the nick of time. Heracles reacts predictably to news of what is going on and makes appropriate plans to rescue his family. All this is well enough worked out, without being startlingly original, though the real affection of Heracles for his sons is perhaps unusual and described in a charming domestic passage:

> They will not let go, but hang upon my clothes all the more. Were you so close to disaster? I will have to lead you as you cling to my hands, like a boat towing her dinghies. (629–32)

Heracles and the boys move off into the palace. Lycus arrives, is tricked into entering, all unawares, and is promptly dispatched. And so the play ought to end. We have already had a completed action, a rescue from adversity, an action of contrasts and reversals, with, as it would seem, a happy conclusion. But the play is only half done. What began as a straightforward suspense story becomes suddenly stark tragedy with the arrival on the palace roof of a *deus*, or rather two *deae*, in the persons of Iris, the messenger of Zeus, and Madness. By the reaction of the Chorus, Madness is a fearsome sight, though she turns out to be reluctant to inflict herself on Heracles. Iris reveals that this is Hera's will and Madness acquiesces, sending out her affliction to make Heracles murder the children. The deities depart and, to the accompanying earthquake, the Chorus dance the madness. The sequence is as striking and shocking as anything in Euripides up to the *Bacchae*, which develops a similar idea and takes it even further.

From here the play returns to a predictable though pathetic path. Mad Heracles, wheeled on like Sophocles' Ajax, tied down until the mania passes, looks forward to Agave in the *Bacchae* as he becomes gradually aware of what he has done. In the final scene with Theseus it is a broken man who has to be helped from the stage. The contrasts are almost perversely harrowing in this savage and moving play, made all the more affecting because it supplies a counterpart to the *Women of Trachis* of Sophocles. There Deianira was a gentle person adrift in a barbaric world. Here Euripides searches out humanity in a man known from myth only by his deeds. Other heroes fall from a position of power and influence, and the fall helps the audience reflect on the vicissitudes of life. Euripides sets up the man of legendary physical prowess and shows the vulnerability of such a man to filial affection, by dramatizing the mental instability which both makes him and breaks him.

A more conventional play would substitute Hera herself, or another god for Iris and Madness, either to open or to close the

play and account for Heracles' derangement. Euripides personi-
fies the breakdown itself, in mid-action, and creates a centre-
piece to the stage action which ultimately dominates the whole.

It is only too easy to use up the vocabulary of tears in
describing Trojan Women, one of several plays which Euripides
located in the aftermath of the war against Troy, matching the
misery of the victims with the inhumanity of the victors. The
scene is placed before the city of Troy, now razed and in ruin.
Here Poseidon, one of the gods who supported the Trojan cause,
opens the play, now bidding the city farewell. He is joined by
Athene, angry at the Greeks' abuse of their victory and seeking
Poseidon's help against them. They agree to render the homecoming of the Greeks as painful as possible.

The setting is outside a tent in which the Trojan prisoners are
being held and, as the play proper begins, Hecuba, the widow of
Priam, king of Troy, laments her fall from queen to slave. Her
personal fate is soon compounded by disasters to her children,
Cassandra doomed to return home with Agamemnon, and
Andromache, whose son Astyanax is hurled over the battle-
ments. In between, Hecuba awards herself the sour compensation of persuading Menelaus to kill Helen as soon as they get
home to Sparta. The play ends with a dirge shared between
Hecuba and the Chorus who give the play its title, they too
destined to become slaves.

That, in brief, is all there is to the play: little conflict, less
plot, no relief from the parade of misery. Only a great
playwright could get away with it, and it is widely regarded as
one of Euripides' masterpieces.

What then lifts it out of a despair almost morbid in its intensity? As ever with Euripides the language supplies a part of the
answer. More, it is the manner in which he concentrates his
purpose in terms of the theatre for which he wrote. The audience for a modern revival needs reminding of the historical
context of the first production, sandwiched, as it was, between
the reduction of Melos for refusing to join the Athenian alliance
in 416 BC and the Sicilian expedition of late 415. Melos was
destroyed, the men massacred, women and children sold into
slavery. From Athens and her allies eighteen months later a
hundred and thirty-four ships set out for Sicily. The force was
virtually wiped out. Euripides may have been in no position to
forecast that débâcle, but no one knew better the seductiveness

of a glorious campaign and the appalling reality of battle.

What *Trojan Women* becomes on stage is a composite view of the effects of war. Poseidon is a Spartan god who forms an alliance with Athene, goddess of Athens, to ensure that in time of war everyone suffers, even the victors. Hecuba's first line 'Raise your battered head from the ground' suggests that the play opens not with the arrival of the gods but with the mortal woman wheeled into position on the *ekkuklema*. While the gods above dispassionately discuss the fate of mankind, the audience are watching the huddled figure below, the individual pain in the face of the historical account and the lists of casualty statistics. This might appear to contravene the practice of detaching the prologue from the main action, but here Euripides does not use a frame plot. Neither god nor goddess returns. What happens instead is that Hecuba remains throughout the rest of the play, including the choral odes. Other characters come and go, but Hecuba is ever-present, it seems, until the whole play ends with her departure accompanied by the Chorus, along the *parodos*, leaving for good her former home. What we have here is the logical extension of concentrating on the individual. Aeschylus immobilized his Prometheus, Sophocles left Creon as a focus to choral ode. Euripides has Hecuba take upon herself the essence of the play as she stands there, or, as often, lies in a state of collapse.

The rest of the characters are all seen in terms of this pathetic creature: the Chorus diffuse and confused, entering perhaps from the *skene* (they say they have come from the tents of Agamemnon) to emphasize their restriction; Talthybius, latterly sympathetic; Cassandra finally ripping away the sacraments of Apollo as the same character does in *Agamemnon* – all these come to Hecuba. So too do Menelaus, Helen, Andromache and her son Astyanax. The scene with Andromache and the child are the most obviously affecting. They are brought in together on a wagon heaped with loot, themselves no more than chattels. The effect of this is allowed to sink in fully before the news leaks out that the child is to die. The scene of farewell between mother and child is all the more touching for Andromache being taken away first as part of the spoils, the child briefly left. This serves to return Hecuba to the centre of attention and it is she who pre-empts the Chorus with a lyric lament after the herald removes Astyanax.

The return of his little body carried on the shield of his father Hector combines in a single action the whole message of the play. War destroys. It destroys cities and soldiers, it destroys homes and families, it destroys the innocent, however young. All here is the result of human folly. No god or goddess is involved in the central action of the play. The play parades butchery in a ruined city, set on fire as a concluding effect to back the final stanzas. What lingers in the mind are those two images, the dead child on the shield, the grandmother left alive while all around her is destroyed.

Electra by contrast is a play with a problem. It faces the critic directly with the question of theatrical values simply because, rightly or wrongly, it is amenable to a psychological interpretation which is consistent and formidably effective, but which may be wholly alien to classical thinking or procedure.

The set provides the first indication that there is something unusual about the play. It is identified by a peasant farmer as his home and both Electra and Orestes comment on its poor appearance. Euripides' concern with visual realism seems well authenticated from Aristophanes' mockery. If, as seems likely, each playwright adapted a basic system of columns, removable units and painted panels to suit his immediate purpose, then a common dwelling could be indicated without stepping beyond the conventions appropriate to setting other plays in the Theatre of Dionysus.

But how was the play acted? Electra and indeed Orestes are given lines and situations where the interpretation of the play hangs absolutely on what is done, rather than on what is said. The outline of the plot is familiar from the treatment of the same story by Aeschylus in the *Oresteia* and Sophocles in his *Electra*, which arguably preceded the Euripides version by a year or two. Clytemnestra has killed her husband Agamemnon and is married to Aegisthus. Orestes, exiled as a baby, returns, and with the help of his sister Electra, executes vengeance on their mother and step-father. Each playwright takes a point of view over the material he is handling, and the very familiarity of the Athenian audience with the story is a stimulus to Euripides. Before the play opens, this Electra has been married off to the peasant in front of whose farm the action takes place. The marriage has not been consummated, but Electra chooses to behave as a proper peasant wife, fetching water and doing the chores. Orestes arrives, but fails to reveal who he is until unmasked by an old shepherd. Aegisthus is killed while acting as host to Orestes and Pylades, Clytemnestra after being tricked into attending Electra as a concerned grandmother. The Farmer speaks the prologue and the Dioscuri arrive at the end to set things straight.

Then the problems start. Electra is still a virgin. The Farmer tells the audience so. Electra talks about it even to the total strangers she believes Orestes and Pylades to be. Is this an ironic contrast in view of her pretended motherhood – the plan she devises to entice her mother – or is it a substantial hint that she is obsessed by sex? Electra sometimes twists the truth, particularly when she is describing her plight. Is this a mark of the oppressed heroine or of the compulsive liar? Does it mean that we should be wary of anything she says in the play which is not corroborated elsewhere? Orestes needs advice on how to proceed with both murders. Is this a playwright's device so that plans may be discussed, or an indication that Orestes is a weak man driven only by his fanatical sister and the implacable Pylades to a course of action contrary to his nature and resolve?

A production necessarily has to come to a decision on all such questions, but a production is not necessarily a means of getting close to Euripides' own intent. One example highlights how important this may be. Orestes first sees Electra early in the play, assumes from her appearance that she is a slave and decides to eavesdrop to discover Electra's whereabouts. Electra enters carrying water from the stream, fails to see Orestes and Pylades, but in a lyric passage of over fifty lines, reveals that she is indeed Electra. What is the accompanying stage action? Orestes and Pylades have hidden themselves, but not so far away as to prevent them barring Electra's path to her door when they emerge from hiding. Does Orestes react to this news that the ragged creature he took to be a slave is the sister he has come to see, or does Pylades? Or is this Pylades the kind of shadowy figure who stands in the background in Aeschylus' *Libation-Bearers*? Orestes now knows who Electra is. He checks up on whether the Chorus are trustworthy and, reassured, neglects to tell Electra who *he* is for another three hundred lines. Now why? The only tolerable answers are either that to do so would damage the plot, which makes Euripides a poor playmaker for whom plausibility takes second place to structural convenience, or that Orestes has decided, after seeing Electra, not to tell her who he is. And the implications of that are far-reaching indeed.

When the old Shepherd arrives, Orestes and Pylades are inside the farmhouse being entertained. Electra comes out to greet him and he offers the news that Orestes must have arrived secretly because someone has visited Agamemnon's grave. Electra dismisses the notion out of hand. The Shepherd then rehearses to Electra the precise recognition symbols by which the Aeschylean Orestes and Electra were united, the lock of hair, footprints and a piece of woven cloth. Electra dismisses them all in the most literal and prosaic of terms as being ridiculous ways of recognizing a brother and sister. At this juncture Orestes emerges from the hut, and the Shepherd identifies him as Orestes by a scar. Orestes confesses who he is and Electra is finally convinced that he is her brother.

This conscious and undeniable evocation of the scene as Aeschylus handled it must provide the key to the play. The audience were asked, indeed forced, to make comparison between the Aeschylus version, perhaps the Sophocles too, and find here in Euripides something new. What is new is an Electra fixated, self-absorbed, demented even, and an Orestes unheroic, hesitant and craven. The rationalist trap is ever-present when dealing with Euripides and it is seductive to read too much into a minor reference. Nevertheless, it is Euripides himself who invites us to contrast his dramatic method with that of former playwrights and the play emerges, not flawed, but as a masterpiece of dramatic consistency in an anti-heroic mould. Orestes is reluctant to identify himself because his sister is not the sister he was expecting. She is reluctant to accept the brother she has found because she had something a great deal more forceful in mind. Orestes is goaded into a murder of Aegisthus which is both savage and unnatural. Euripides gives to Clytemnestra as many cards as he can muster and her murder at the hands of her children is sheer butchery, unjustified and unjustifiable. The Dioscuri, who sort things out, make the most vivid of contrasts between the demands of the myth up above, as they appear on the *mechane*, and the reality of domestic murder featured at stage level.

Such a concluding visual contrast between myth and reality can be found in a number of Euripides' plays, becoming almost his signature. The *Bacchae* completes the idea. As in *Medea* a principal character, Dionysus, becomes his own *deus ex machina*, but whereas in *Medea* the name character is promoted to godhead almost in defiance of the way she has behaved, the Dionysus of *Bacchae* is from the outset both god and man.

Opening the play Dionysus identifies himself to the audience as a god 'disguised as a man'. Although a passage from the conclusion is missing from the manuscripts, it would appear that he returns in epiphany at the end. The regular frame is fractured by having the humans challenge and reject his behaviour, while the Chorus who give the play its title keep faith with him.

The close-knit family ties within the house of Cadmus are central to a play which contains so many original and disturbing elements that some may be overlooked. Dionysus is aggrieved that he is accepted neither as the son of Zeus, nor as the son of Agave, his earthly mother. The human part of him is isolated from his family, the godly part gives him his supernatural power. The family of Cadmus, to which he lays claim, are not without fault. Pentheus, the king, is young, puritanical and ill-equipped to cope with the crisis he faces. But it is his affection for his grandfather Cadmus which causes him to turn on Teiresias and berate him for making the old man look foolish in public. Both in this early scene and when he returns with Pentheus' body, Cadmus is overwhelmed by love for his grandson and for his daughter Agave. The final scene demonstrates this in stage terms with the god above, cut off from the human contact his human half both craves and rejects.

The other part of Dionysus is the supernatural nature of his attributes. God of the vine, god of ecstasy, god of the irrational, his power is fearsome. In *Madness of Heracles* the hero is afflicted by Madness personified, and Madness is directed at the whim of Hera. Dionysus wields a similar power, but he wields it himself. The maenads in the mountains have no understanding of what they do. Pentheus is driven out of his mind once Dionysus has exerted his influence. Madness exists as a sickness, but Dionysus is something more than this. It is through the Chorus that the playwright gives the religion concrete form.

The Chorus of the *Bacchae* is arguably the supreme theatrical notion in the whole of Greek drama. The play concerns the arrival in Thebes of the Dionysiac religion. Pentheus, king of Thebes, and Dionysus' cousin, opposes it. Dionysus destroys him. Dionysus has come from Asia, leading a troupe of female followers, the Bacchae of the title, who form the Chorus. Pentheus is not aware of who Dionysus is, nor does the god reveal himself even when Pentheus has him arrested. Instead he begins to exert his 'hypnotic' influence over the king and persuades him to dress up as a woman in order to go and witness the Bacchic rites on the mountainside. These rites are being performed by the women of Thebes, led by Pentheus' mother, Agave, and his aunts. The women catch Pentheus and, thinking that he is a lion, tear him to bits. This is, of course, reported by a Messenger, but Agave returns to the stage, carrying her son's head on her Bacchic wand, to be gradually restored by Cadmus to sanity and a full understanding of what she has done.

In such a macabre plot there are inevitably shocks: the grotesque sight of Cadmus and Teiresias decked out as Bacchants, the one almost too old to walk propping up his blind friend in a sequence more in keeping with the mid-twentieth-century vision of a Beckett or a de Ghelderode; the confrontation of Pentheus, the soldier, and Dionysus, the god, effeminate in appearance with long hair and a smiling mask; an earthquake during the course of which Dionysus claims to destroy the palace; Pentheus, dressed as a woman, primping across the stage, wondering anxiously whether his seams are straight; Agave brandishing aloft her son's head under the impression that it is a lion's while the rest of the torn body lies at her feet. All these sequences contribute to the play's power. But the Chorus is the religion itself personified. In their song, in their dance, in their reaction to the events the Chorus *demonstrate* Dionysus in all his aspects: the miraculous, the escapist, the ecstatic and the orgiastic.

It cannot have escaped the reader's notice that the performance tradition that I first proposed based on a forceful and graphic chorus has undergone a major change of emphasis in the works of Sophocles and Euripides. The choruses of these later playwrights may still have contributed to both the tenor and the appearance of the total performance, but the centre of attention has moved away from the *orchestra* with its group patterns to the individual responses which the third actor encouraged. Discussing some of the plays of Sophocles and Euripides I have virtually ignored the chorus, beyond assuming that they have maintained a flexible nature and responded in movement to moments of conflict or the varieties of tension around which plays are constructed.

Quite possibly this underestimates how involved each chorus was during the latter part of the fifth century BC. The manner in which Euripides handles the chorus in *Bacchae*, his last play, makes it plain that a visually dominant chorus had been, by the most conservative estimate, no more than dormant.

Each choral ode in the *Bacchae* is designed to reveal some aspect of the religion and the corporate nature of the Dionysiac experience is perfectly matched to the form of the tragic chorus. Many Euripidean choruses display an attitude to the characters and events which may be taken to reflect those of the playwright. Others are confused, ambivalent or just plain irrelevant. In *Electra* the Chorus seem to change sides, their sympathy for Electra evaporating in the face of her actions. Only in the *Bacchae* are they the vibrant, pulsating entity found in Aeschylus. To suggest that Euripides returns to the Aeschylean model for his chorus of Bacchants is to over-simplify. The Aeschylean chorus may regularly have reflected in reaction the speeches of the principals and, in so doing, directed the attitude of the audience. In the *Bacchae* the Chorus are the embodiment of the religion's amorality in all its seductiveness. When Pentheus threatens to sell off the Chorus into slavery in order 'to still their drums and cymbals', it is far more than a vague acknowledgement of their presence before him as he tries to deal with Dionysus. It is the clearest of indications that during the preceding scene, and in all probability since their first entrance with Dionysus, they have provided a rhythmic accompaniment to the scenes behind them. It may be beyond proof to suggest that they seethe when the King berates Teiresias, become conspirators as Dionysus coaxes Pentheus out of his wits, gloat over the gory description of his death and even yield briefly towards sympathy for the stricken Agave. It is hardly fanciful. If Pentheus pays them scant attention as they rattle and rave about his courtyard, this is less of an indication that their contribution to what is going on is insignificant than an affirmation of the chorus as stage device in Greek drama. As the living, pulsating hydra that was the religion itself, Euripides presents an idea so striking as to be inimitable. Never again was the chorus to be such a force in the drama.

8

EURIPIDES:
THE COMEDIES

Euripides did not write any comedies, if comedy is to be defined by Aristotelian principles, or by festival entry. In Athens the genres were strictly segregated. Plato has no difficulty in getting his disputants in the *Republic* to agree that the same man cannot write as well both tragedy and comedy, or indeed perform in both. The corollary is that an actor can only play one part well, which renders the whole argument philosophical rather than aesthetic, but we may take it that no playwright of the classical period did write and submit both tragedies and old comedies of the Aristophanic kind. But there were also the satyr plays which tragic playwrights did present. The satyr play had been the fourth in any tetralogy from earliest times. A direct link between the plays of a submission died out during the fifth century BC, but the satyr play held its place. Only in the fourth century was it detached from its traditional position and performed, sometimes first in a group, sometimes in isolation, at local festivals which had sanctioned their own pattern of performance.

The satyr play was a brief burlesque treatment of a subject from mythology. It seems to have had sufficient similarities to old comedy, as represented for posterity exclusively by the works of Aristophanes, for it to be a little surprising that the Athenian playwrights should so readily accept the compartment into which they were slotted, but our evidence is slim. Only one complete satyr play has survived, the *Cyclops* of Euripides, and half of Sophocles' *Ichneutae*. *Cyclops* is on a Homeric theme, its humour Homeric too in that it concentrates on physical discomfort.

Extant Aeschylus shows little light relief, yet Aeschylus had the reputation of writing the best of satyr plays. In the theatre, of course, humour is something far wider than the writing of funny lines. It may be that many of those bland and non-committal interjections which so many choruses present between major oratorical speeches were considered 'humorous' in so far as they reflected the audience's appreciation of argument and anticipated a character's reply. The rhythm of a play is a fluctuating thing which playwright, director and actors manipulate. At first sight Greek tragedy can seem unrelieved in its intensity, but it does not require a great deal of sensitivity to appreciate that in any Greek play the balance of action and discourse is carefully weighed and that the location of incident within a choral framework is consciously crafted. By all modern criteria the Greeks made plays well.

Aeschylus does allow for changes of tempo and lightness of touch, even if the introduction of a character such as the Nurse in *Libation-Bearers* is exceptional. The *Oresteia* does after all have a triumphal ending. The *Prometheia* perhaps did too, and the *Danaid* tetralogy. So without a doubt did *Persians*, for an Athenian audience.

Sophocles developed the wry smile of recognition, the ironic touch which enables the audience to evaluate a moment by reference to their own superior knowledge. This was one of the bases of Sophocles' theatrical method at its strongest and is demonstrated in incidents such as the concealing of the body of Clytemnestra under the sheet in *Electra*, staged less in the interest of the plot than of sheer theatrical *élan*.

Euripides picked up and elaborated this aspect of the macabre. Perhaps he even taught it to Sophocles. Two of the plays considered in the last chapter give notable examples.

The recognition scene in *Electra* has Orestes unmasked by the old Shepherd, whose arrival he had never expected. The dialogue indicates the action:

ORESTES: Electra, whose friend is this antique relic of mankind?

ELECTRA: This is the man, stranger, who brought up my father.

ORESTES: What are you saying? Is this the man who hid away your brother?

ELECTRA: This is the man who saved him, if he does still live.

ORESTES: Oh. Why is he staring at me like someone examining the hallmark on a piece of silver? Does he think I resemble someone?

ELECTRA: Perhaps he's glad to see a friend of Orestes.

ORESTES: Yes, Orestes is my friend. But why is he circling round me?

ELECTRA: I am amazed too, stranger, seeing what he is doing.

SHEPHERD: Daughter Electra, my mistress, pray to the gods. . . (553–64)

Orestes' unwillingness to face the old man is a pointer to his anxiety about how matters are developing, to such an extent that the eventual greeting of brother and sister some fifteen lines later has acquired a comic subtext of mutual dismay.

Orestes contains an unusual sequence involving the same character but with a different personality. As part of the plot hatched against Helen and Hermione, Electra enters the palace. The Chorus hear cries which they attempt to drown and a Messenger arrives to tell those outside what has just taken place indoors. But this Messenger is a Phrygian slave whose Greek is as pidgin as that of the Scythian in Aristophanes' *Women at the Thesmophoria* and barely more intelligible than that of the Triballian in *Frogs*, who speaks such gobbledygook that his companions can both claim that he means exactly what they want him to mean. The translation, though not literal, gives the flavour of the terrified Phrygian's speech:

Argive sword try kill me. Fled from death I have, in Turkish slippers. Up and over roof clamber. Chop, chop. Squeeze between roof-beams. Come, go. Down come. Where go? Whoops. Help. Where go now, ladies? (1369–76)

He can hardly but have looked comic, making his entrance, it would seem, climbing over the roof of the *skene*. The tale he has to tell is of mayhem and miracle within the palace. No sooner has he finished than Orestes arrives, to taunt the poor man who by this time is gibbering with terror. Orestes cracks a few grizzly jokes at his expense before releasing him. That the scene shows Orestes in a poor light by even the most callous of standards can hardly be denied, but that the slave himself is a comic figure is just as sure. Nor is this the only comic effect in a play which is notable for an elaborate in-joke at the expense of the tragic chorus.

The opening confrontation of the play between Electra and Helen is conducted across the sleeping figure of Orestes, who has suffered a kind of brainstorm in the wake of the murder of his mother. Helen leaves the stage with her daughter Hermione just as Electra catches sight of the Chorus arriving. Anxious in case Orestes should wake up, Electra tries to prevent them behaving like a chorus: 'Quietly, my friends. Gently, please. Not a sound, not a whisper.' The Chorus respond, 'Here we go, tiptoeing along.' 'Get away from his bed', implores Electra. 'Right you are. We obey', they sing. 'Your music is too loud.' 'No more than a whisper.' So the scene proceeds with Electra trying to get these twelve noisy women to leave the stage entirely, which, being the Chorus, they cannot do, until, with a sudden outburst of concern that Orestes is so quiet he may have died, they wake him up.

The point to be made is that Euripides' sympathy to mood is not a little coloured by a taste for the grotesque. This, allied to his relish for the conscious artificiality of the stage, makes him seem, of the three tragedians, the one most in tune with a twentieth-century sensibility and a theatre 'of protest and paradox'.

To allow that there are comic elements in certain, if not all, of Euripides' dramas is not the same as to suggest that such plays as *Electra* and *Orestes* are predominantly comedies. There are five whose tone is so light-hearted, if not frivolous, that they can be considered at least as 'romances' for the sake of another label. In these the comic element virtually eliminates even tragic potential. That one of them is the satyr play *Cyclops* while another, *Alcestis*, was presented in the satyr position in a submission of four, betrays perhaps a certain frustration on the part of Euripides that the festival categories were as rigid as he found them.

Short and consciously absurd, the satyr play *Cyclops* may be unique to us, but was probably not untypical of the genre. The prime aim of the satyr play was to give a respite to the audience and presumably to the performers, by concluding the diet of three consecutive tragedies with a comic piece, linked in theme and sometimes in plot, as the titles of the many lost plays bear witness. A serious occasion, therefore, ended on a note of buffoonery.

No more is known about the staging of the satyr play than about that of tragedy or comedy, but a number of vase illustrations indicate that theatrical contrast arose from juxtaposing serious characters and a potentially serious situation with the ludicrous antics of the satyr chorus, its leader Silenus, and, on occasions, Dionysus himself. *Cyclops'* plot follows the line prescribed by Homer in the *Odyssey* with Odysseus and his men captured by the one-eyed Polyphemus and escaping by making him drunk and then blinding him. The Homeric joke of Odysseus calling himself 'Noman' stays, but is exploited as a means for the Chorus to mock Polyphemus rather than as an illustration of Odysseus' cunning in preventing the Cyclops from getting help from his fellows.

Sheep present a problem. Polyphemus is a shepherd and the justification for the presence of the satyrs in the first place is that they have been ship-wrecked and are now being forced to assist him. So their leader Silenus tells the audience in the prologue. When the rest of the Chorus enter a few lines later, they are 'driving' their flocks before them:

> Who cares about your pedigree? Where are you off to, wandering over the rocks?. . .get down here at once, you horny thing. . .stop gorging and get in the cave. (41 ff.)

The entrance of the Chorus was clearly some kind of dance and the sheep were either real, or imaginary, or represented in some way. Strangely, Silenus calls his satyrs to order when he sees Odysseus and the Greeks, leaving the 'sheep' to attendants. Whether these attendants are in character wearing costume and mask, or stand outside the action as 'invisible' stage managers is not known. The other conventions of the stage could accommodate either alternative in tragedy or satyr, but why should these attendants have been needed in the first place in *Cyclops*? If the sheep were actors dressed in fleeces, they could quite comfortably have got themselves off into the cave. If they were not present at all and the Chorus simply mimed their existence, then anything that attendants could do would confuse rather than clarify the issue. One is left, by default, with the proposition that the Chorus of satyrs entered driving real sheep and that sufficient attendants were also present to shepherd them off when no longer required.

The end of the play seems to confirm that this was the original intention. In Homer Odysseus and his men get out of the cave by clinging to the underside of the sheep as they emerge from the cave, because Polyphemus is sitting at the entrance to prevent the men from escaping. In Euripides the Chorus trick him into moving away from the entrance. The Homeric scene could have been staged with sheep/actors, but never with real sheep. Euripides' decision to ignore a familiar element of the original is perhaps dictated by the fact that it cannot be staged with the resources he is using and that, therefore, he has to manage his cave exit in some other way.

Elsewhere in the play there are two devices which, if not original, emphasize the closeness of satyric to tragic practice and confirm a pattern in Euripides' stage technique. At the moment when Odysseus arrives with his men, he recognizes the setting as a cave and the group standing around as satyrs. What he does not know is where he and his men have been shipwrecked. So he asks Silenus:

> ODYSSEUS: What is this place? Who lives here?
> SILENUS: That's Etna, highest mountain in Sicily.
> ODYSSEUS: Where are the walls, and the towers of the city?
> SILENUS: There aren't any. It's deserted here, Stranger.
> ODYSSEUS: No men at all? Or only wild animals?
> SILENUS: There are Cyclopses, living in caves not houses with roofs. (113-18)

Other plays have made use of the setting, drawing attention to it in a way that suggests that location was indicated by emblematic rather than representational means. *Cyclops* predates Sophocles' *Philoctetes*, in which the cave of the protagonist is described in detail. What Euripides appears to be doing is making fun of the form of setting. Odysseus draws attention to the stage set and the difference between a cave and a house with a roof because of their similarity. The theatrical in-joke is reinforced when the Cyclops arrives and Silenus urges the Greeks to hide in the cave. Odysseus expostulates, saying that they will all be trapped, and confronts the Cyclops, only to be driven inside with his men. In ensuing scenes Odysseus comes and goes from the cave whenever he wants to, though the rest of the Greeks are apparently unable to do so. The occasion dictates its own logic, just as the 'giant' Cyclops was played by an actor, even if reinforced and with specialist mask. His size could never have been so great as to defy the concerted attack of Odysseus and his men, or indeed swing a man round by his heels and knock his brains out, the fate of some of Odysseus' companions, as he reveals on one of his excursions from backstage. This is nothing to do with the sophistication – or lack of it – of any Greek audience. It is a simple matter of the logic of Christmas pantomime.

On occasions the language of *Cyclops*, and of the large fragment which we possess of Sophocles' *Ichneutae*, is rather fine and the sentiments serious. Odysseus' recitation of the fate of his men has qualities of some of the better Messenger speeches. Odysseus talks to the Cyclops of the horrors of war in sentiments which, in the context of late fifth-century Athens, could seem sensitive, while the Cyclops' devotion to his own interest, 'the wise man's god is Wealth', sounds like something more than the rambling of a cardboard ogre.

What Euripides may have been creating in his satyr play is a serious theme, made farcical only by the antics of the Chorus. When the Cyclops is blinded and wanders about, bumping into the set ('Cyclops, you look terrible'), for all the callous jokes, it is difficult not to be reminded of Oedipus who tore out his own eyes, or Polymestor, savaged by Hecuba and her women. The argument in favour of dating *Cyclops* to the same group of plays as *Hecuba* is difficult to support from external evidence, but that the two post-blinding scenes were linked is plausible. A violent event is pathetic or comic *because* of the Chorus reaction to it. To accept this is to open the door to the satyr play being something far more subtle than a vulgar romp to take the audience's minds off the sad events of the tragedies they have witnessed. It was an opportunity to consider the distorted view of human endeavour and to reflect from a different angle on the futility of human aspirations, an opportunity which the playwrights welcomed. This would fit well with Euripides' experimentation with the form of the fourth submission in a group of plays.

Alcestis is the earliest extant play of Euripides and it ought to be a satyr play. It was presented in 438 BC, last in a group of four plays of which the most renowned in Euripides' own time was *Telephus*. *Telephus* was the play in which Euripides chose to dress his beggar king as a beggar rather than as a king, a novelty which Aristophanes seized upon gleefully. But *Telephus* is lost and for whatever reason *Alcestis* survived alone.

The play concerns King Admetus of Pherae, who did Apollo a good turn and was rewarded by being allowed to cheat death when his time came, naming another in his place. Euripides' play opens with Apollo trying to persuade Death not to take Admetus' wife Alcestis, who has volunteered to die in his stead. It soon becomes clear that Euripides' interest in the subject revolves around the question of what sort of benefit Apollo has really bestowed. Admetus has trotted round all his friends and relations in search of a substitute, not surprisingly without success, before his wife agrees to die for him. What sort of a man would accept such an offer becomes the pivot for the remainder of the piece. Only after Alcestis' death does Admetus come to realize what he has done. He is then too ashamed to admit it to Heracles who arrives as a guest. A servant reveals the truth to the roistering Heracles, who sobers up quickly enough when he hears what has happened. Heracles resolves to help, successfully wrestles with Death for Alcestis and, in a marvellously wrought final scene, tests Admetus' new-found self-awareness with a veiled Alcestis who is eventually restored to her husband.

The play is a fable, a humane and touching fable, akin in mood to *The Winter's Tale*, though far less ambitious. Any attempt, and several have been made, to suggest that the play has satyric elements to justify its fourth position in a group submission, are unconvincing, but it is not difficult to see that fourth was the only place in which Euripides could try out a new kind of drama. *Alcestis* is no satyr play, still less is it old comedy in the Aristophanic mould. Nor is it tragedy, for all its tragic potential, any more than *The Winter's Tale* deserves the same 'label' as *Othello*.

For the Jacobean audience this was not particularly important, for the Greek it was. In 438 BC there was, it seems, no place for the playwright to experiment in form outside the rigid categories of festival entry. *Alcestis* can pass today, if label must be found, as 'tragi-comedy', 'romance' or simply 'drama'. For Euripides, writing in the fifth century BC, it represents the first move towards a new kind of drama, a drama which made room for the comic elements in *Electra* and *Orestes* and which led to the positively light-hearted 'tragedies' such as *Helen* and *Ion*.

Alcestis should be taken on its own terms rather than as the satyr play it patently is not. *Telephus* was remembered for its costume detail and costume is an element in *Alcestis* as well. Apollo and Death carry emblems, a bow and a sword. Heracles tells us that Death is dressed in black. The visual contrast of mourning black and normal clothes is one that keeps recurring throughout the play. Soon after the play opens the Chorus arrive from the town, confused about what is happening. They know that this is the day when Alcestis is expected to die, but they do not know if she is yet dead. They look and listen for signs, but it is clear from the later text that they are not yet wearing mourning. Alcestis, when she is wheeled out – she dies on-stage – is wearing her finest clothes. As soon as the body has been removed inside, Admetus decrees public mourning without music, a novel effect for subsequent choral odes perhaps. Black is to be worn. Heads, and even the manes of the horses, are to be shorn.

By the time that Heracles arrives, the Chorus have not had the opportunity to go off and change. Heracles does notice that Admetus is dressed in mourning, but Admetus cannot bring himself to tell his friend what has happened in case he refuses to stay. Heracles is welcomed into the palace, Admetus having told him that his mourning is for a distant relative only. As attendants prepare to carry the corpse to the funeral, Admetus' old father Pheres arrives, also dressed in black. A disgraceful squabble takes place between the two men, conducted across the body, to which their costume at least suggests they should be paying respect.

I have already noted how unusual it is to encounter an empty stage in Greek tragedy. It is possible that there is an example here, for the Chorus could depart with the bier. The point is important in the present argument because, if they do depart, it is reasonable to assume that when they return they too are wearing black, so that the series of contrasts can be multiplied up to the resolution. If they stay at this point, they become privy to Heracles' plan to confront Death and, at least for them, the unveiling of Alcestis can be no surprise. Heracles discovers who has really died when a servant reproves his drunkenness, 'You could see our hair and black garments', and the over-shadowing of the whole scene in black, as each new character enters, is part of the series of antitheses which Euripides has set up.

Heracles departs to fight Death and returns with Alcestis, her head covered so that Admetus may not recognize her until Heracles has tested him and discovered that he does indeed deserve his wife back. The stage picture dominated by funereal black gives a nice contrast to the contrived, though charming, happy ending.

The death of Alcestis is significant, not for its public nature, death on stage being less of a taboo than most commentators would have us believe, but for the way it transfers emphasis to her husband. Admetus, whose every speech in the first part is self-centred, is forced to listen to his wife's dying words. Instead of the long speech we might expect from him, however, as Alcestis breathes her last, there is a pause while their young son Eumelus sings two lyric passages. Here the potential tragedy is dominant, not in the loss to Admetus of the wife he 'killed', but to the child of a loving mother. The words sung are unimportant. It is the young voice which makes them poignant. For the first time, but not the last, Euripides reveals the true pathos of a family destroyed by Death.

With similar skill he restores the family, again as echoed in *The Winter's Tale*, in God's good time, and when mankind has learnt from its mistakes. The contrast of strength and weakness usually found in the person of Heracles is muted here, but the theme is there, subordinated on this occasion to a portrait of a family restored. *Alcestis* is a fine antidote to those who see Euripides only as the playwright of despair.

Iphigeneia in Tauris is more of a *Cymbeline* with its air of having been assembled out of half a dozen other pieces of Euripides. Compared to *Alcestis* it has far more comic sequences, and the mixture of romance and realism makes for a good adven-ture story. The outcome is a happy one for the protagonists, and the thwarted King Thoas, by no stretch of the imagination a vil-lain, is easily reconciled by Athene to the loss of his statue of Artemis, his priestess, two sacrificial victims and his entire chorus.

The plotline follows the fortunes of Agamemnon's daughter Iphigeneia, who was spirited away at the moment the sacrificial knife was heading for her neck on the altar at Aulis. Miraculously preserved, she has been dumped in the Crimea as priestess of Artemis with the task of ensuring that all visitors are murdered. Her opening speech catalogues the miseries of such a life and there is little indication that the mood of the play will change. Iphigeneia retreats indoors to be replaced by Orestes and Pylades who enter apprehensively. Pylades is the more resolute of the two, a substantial character who spurns retreat when Orestes wants to run off and hide in a cave at the sight of the blood-stained altar and the trophies of the slain. To state that the opening echoes the early scenes of *Electra* begs the question as to which of the plays was written first. There is no real evidence, but there is some agreement that the two plays were written at about the same time, perhaps even in the same year. There would be a thematic point in this, as the reason for Orestes' and Pylades' arrival relates to the murder of Clytemnestra. After the trial of Orestes on the Areopagus, some of the Furies have rejected the verdict. Orestes has sought refuge yet again with Apollo, threatening a hunger strike, and Apollo has pronounced, somewhat arbitrarily, that Orestes will finally be free if he can steal a wooden image of Artemis from the temple of the Taurians and take it to Attica. Orestes is still being pursued by the Furies and his subsequent capture on the beach is in part due to suffering a fit, during which he attacks the cattle of the local herdsmen.

Brought before Iphigeneia for sacrifice, Orestes is revealed to his sister. Together they hatch an escape plot whose similarity to the conclusion of *Helen*, usually dated at 412 BC, must be caused by something more than mere paucity of imagination on the part of the author. In such circumstances it is difficult to resist speculating that there were positive links between all three plays, or that their thematic connection was somehow reflected in performance. The linguistic and metrical echoes are sufficiently regular to suggest proximate dates, were all other evidence lacking. A common sentiment about the destructiveness of war and the haphazard nature of fate can be traced more closely than in the rest of Euripides' work in which such sentiments feature. Perhaps, too, something should be made out of the curious emphasis on the physical features of the set in the *Iphigeneia in Tauris*. To Orestes it presents a formidable obstacle, but Pylades spies a gap between the triglyphs by means of which they might be able to break into the palace. Then there is the curious device of the letter which Iphigeneia had written long ago to be delivered to her brother and whose contents she recites to Pylades, in case he is shipwrecked and loses it in his escape. Even Aristotle, whose sense of theatre left something to be desired, commented on the incongruity of Orestes' reaction to this in a recognition scene overdrawn to the point of parody.

Yet behind such references the playwright is at work drawing attention, in humorous fashion, to the romantic core of the play. By the time that Orestes and his sister meet, all tragic potential has gone by the board. In *Electra* Orestes tries to avoid being recognized once he has discovered the true nature of his sister. Here in *Iphigeneia in Tauris*, the recognition is a suspense sequence, but laughable rather than painful. The Herdsman who tells of the capture of the Greeks has heard one of them called Pylades and, after a lament by Iphigeneia for her home and her brother, the Chorus announce the arrival of the two men in chains. Iphigeneia's reaction is to wonder who Orestes is and who his parents were. Orestes for his part wonders who Iphigeneia can be to be so concerned about a couple of strangers. Three hundred lines later Iphigeneia quotes the letter she has handed to Pylades which reads, 'Tell Orestes this is a greeting from someone he has assumed dead'. It then takes Orestes another twenty lines to reach the point at which Pylades fondly introduces him to his sister. In between they all get as close to revealing who they really are as it is possible to get without actually discovering the truth.

IPHIGENEIA: What name did your father give you?

ORESTES: I should really be called Unfortunate.

IPHIGENEIA: Still, I ask this. Tell me in the name of Good Fortune.

ORESTES: If I die nameless, I die unmocked.

IPHIGENEIA: Why will you not tell me? Are you too important?

ORESTES: You shall sacrifice my body, not my name. . . .

IPHIGENEIA: What news of (Achilles) the son of Thetis?

ORESTES: He is dead. His wedding, planned at Aulis turned out otherwise.

IPHIGENEIA: A deception, as those who suffered know.
  (499 ff.)

And so it proceeds with Pylades and Orestes left alone to specu-
late.

ORESTES: By the gods, Pylades, are you thinking what I'm
  thinking?
PYLADES: I do not know. You ask without telling me what
  you are thinking. (657–8)

When Orestes finally accepts that Iphigeneia is his sister, it is
left to the Chorus to cap what cannot help being played as a
comic sequence with the sentiment, 'Whoever you are,
Stranger, keep your hands off her sacred costume'. Another
forty lines and Iphigeneia is convinced.

It is difficult to resist the impression that Euripides felt that
the stock of tragic recognitions had been well and truly
exhausted, and had reacted by taking the audience along with
the story. The impression is reinforced by the handling of a
similar sequence in *Helen*. Is this parody? Pastiche rather, in
that it can only be performed in accordance with the means of
presentation of tragedy, and certainly without the grotesquerie
of the satyr play. At the same time it gives a sense almost of
period charm to the devices, for so long the climactic moments
of high seriousness. Nor is it destructive in intent. What
Euripides offers from out of the confusion of this recognition
scene in *Iphigeneia in Tauris* is the feeling of genuine affection,
so conspicuously absent from *Electra* and *Orestes*, in which
hatred and envy dominate every domestic act. Iphigeneia loves
her brother; Orestes and Pylades are models of loyalty and affection; Pylades is in love with the Electra he has left back home.
The play is pervaded by warmth. Even Thoas, king of the
Taurians, is described as a kind man, and it is only primitive
custom which keeps him massacring interlopers.

It is in overall mood rather than verbal humour that the
comedy of *Iphigeneia in Tauris* resides, but there is one
sequence in which pure farce takes over. Iphigeneia, Orestes
and Pylades plan, with the tacit support of the Chorus, to trick
Thoas into providing an escape boat by suggesting that Orestes
can only be sacrificed out at sea because he is a matricide. 'By
Apollo', says Thoas, wide-eyed, 'not the sort of thing a barbarian
would risk'. He is quick enough to wonder how Iphigeneia can

know that the strangers are unfit to be sacrificed. She improvises: 'The image of the goddess turned on its plinth'. 'By itself', asks cunning Thoas, 'or did an earthquake do it?' 'By itself', she replies, and as a clincher, 'and it winked too'. That seals it. Iphigeneia gives orders for the sacred procession and Thoas acquiesces in every detail, including that nobody shall watch what is going on. The two victims are to have their heads covered in a cloth. All the locals are to go indoors in case they get polluted and even Thoas is to shield his face in his sleeve. So the procession moves off, the wooden image of Artemis, the one that winked, held aloft and all the actors with averted gaze, declining from the truth. It is yet another example of the power-ful image, this time a real image turned into a comic stage image, climaxing a play whose main theme is that of family affection in conflict with blind religious prejudice.

Helen, similar in so many ways, also starts with the after-effects of a shipwreck. Menelaus and his men, on the way back from Troy, are washed up in Egypt and arrive at the court of King Theoclymenus, who is also in the habit of executing passing Greeks. As it happens, this is where Helen has spent the ten years of the Trojan War, because this play is based on a version of the myth which had Paris taking off to Troy a look-alike of Helen, fashioned out of *aether*, while the real one languished in Egypt, blameless despite the importuning of the insistent Theoclymenus. Husband and wife meet, recognize one another after an upset or two and plan their escape with the help of the king's sister Theonoe. They trick the king into believing that Menelaus has been lost at sea and that various Greek rites must be performed for him from on board ship. The gullible Theoclymenus agrees to give them a boat. The ending is not so far different from *Iphigeneia in Tauris*, except that the king is eventually persuaded to accept what has happened by Castor, Helen's brother, whereas in the other play it is Athene who convinces Thoas to live with his loss.

Helen used to affront critics by being so blatantly comic, despite its tragic form, and a number of apologists have con-cluded that it must have been composed for private perfor-mance, rather than for the public theatre. Less rigid scholarship allows the play on its own terms and rejoices in the playwright enjoying himself and making fun of his own dramatic technique. That there is a serious underlying point cannot be denied. If the image of the twitchy wooden goddess in *Iphigeneia in Tauris* is an encouragement to an audience to wink back at her, the notion of a phantom beauty for whom a ten-year war was fought is as precise and absurdist as any in the drama. Nor should we forget that Menelaus and Helen only escape by killing off an uncomfortably large number of Theoclymenus' troops while leaving Theonoe to face her brother's fury. But all ends happily and the dramatic process from exposition to resolution offers a series of enchanting ideas and inventions.

Elsewhere in Greek drama Helen receives a pretty bad press, perhaps the reason why Euripides chose to pick up the Hesiod variant on the myth, which protects her reputation. The Helen who opens the play is not only virtuous, she is thoroughly sceptical about all the stories told of her background: '. . .if the story is reliable', she appends to the story of the reputed seduction of her mother Leda by Zeus in the guise of a swan. And in an outburst to the Chorus:

> Didn't my mother bear me as a portent to mankind? No other woman, Greek or foreigner, hatched children from a shell the way my mother Leda did for Zeus, so they say. (257–9)

When first Teucer and then Helen's husband Menelaus arrive, Euripides can exploit the potential of such scepticism. The general assumption that Helen has been in Troy rather than Egypt is built up almost as a 'running gag', a joke which grows by repetition, here enhanced by a standard of the comic actor's repertoire, the 'double take'. Teucer enters immediately after Helen's prologue and is preoccupied, as so many of the characters are in Euripides' plays, by admiring the setting. Suddenly he sees Helen. 'Ah. Ye gods. What's this I see? The bloody likeness of the most hated of women'. In this initial variant on the recognition, Teucer thinks he recognizes Helen, but she does not know him. Teucer then decides he must have made a mistake and, encouraged by Helen, decides that she merely looks like Helen. The reason for Teucer's presence is principally to let Helen, and incidentally the audience, know what has been happening elsewhere, but this is not purely functional. The value of the scene resides in its supplying the first part of a pattern of scepticism about appearances. The deceptiveness of what the gods may provide for man becomes skilfully wedded to the basic artifice of stage presentation. Teucer departs, reassured that Helen is not Helen, to be replaced by Menelaus, Helen's husband. Helen meanwhile has retreated into the palace and misses the entrance of this incongruous figure. By his own admission Menelaus does not look the way he ought to:

> For I have neither food nor clothes for my body. You can tell from these tatters I am wearing, washed up from the ship. As for the nice shiny costume I had before, the sea's got it. (420–4)

The joke about Euripides dressing his kings in rags is familiar enough, but here we have Euripides apparently drawing attention to Menelaus' state of undress. Every new character to enter comments on it, six references in all. The anti-heroic aspect of Menelaus is matched by an encounter with a *concierge* who threatens to throw him out – 'Where are my famous armies now?' he mutters crossly – and a series of impractical plans of escape when Helen has finally accepted him, which she tactfully fields before coming up with a practical proposition.

The build-up of stage contrasts is conducted at several levels within the play. What Menelaus looks like and how he is treated clearly contribute to the central purpose, but principally as a part of the 'recognition'. When Helen first encounters Menelaus she does not know him because of his appearance. Menelaus is unwilling to recognize her because he is not expecting to see her:

MENELAUS: Gracious. Who are you? Whose face do I see?
HELEN: Who are you? You took the words out of my mouth.
MENELAUS: I never saw anybody more like. . . . (557–9)

Menelaus takes a deal of persuading. Helen is relieved to hear that his 'other' wife is also Helen, but as Menelaus says, 'My eyes could be deceiving me, and I do have another wife'. The scene is a delight to which the odd quotation can do little service. It concludes with a Messenger arriving, apprehensive, as well he might be, about having to tell his master that the Helen in the cave has dissolved in a puff of smoke. Twelve lines into his prepared piece, he breaks off with the biggest double take yet: 'Oh. Hello, daughter of Leda, you were here then, were you?'.

The recurrent jokes are built around the same theme. The

king's sister Theonoe is a prophetess who 'knows everything'. She enters at the head of a solemn procession before turning to Helen with the words 'What do my prophecies say now? Menelaus has arrived. That is him, standing in front of you'. The whole progress of plot and escape are lighthearted enough, developing, as they do, variations on the theme of appearance and disappearance upon which the play is founded. The king is deceived without difficulty and is so furious when he finds out that he has to be restrained by a Servant, perhaps even by the Chorus, from rushing into the palace to kill his sister, whose complicity he appreciates. And the Dioscuri arrive above to set things to rights and end the play on a suitable note of reconciliation.

Helen is comic, not only in its tone and romantic framework, but in its dialogue and situation. Like the greatest of the world's comedies, it contains much serious matter about human relationships and all is set in a stage world both inventive and intelligent. Though wrought from myth, it is a true forerunner of the social comedy of the following century, though perhaps less so than the last play to be considered here.

The plot of *Ion* is complicated. As a young woman Creusa was raped and gave birth to a child whom she exposed. Many years later she comes to Delphi intent on discovering what happened to the child. She is now married to Xuthus who knows nothing about this child and has brought her so that the oracle may tell them why they are childless. The oracle informs Xuthus that the first person he meets when he leaves the sanctuary will be his son. The first person he meets is Ion, a foundling brought up as a temple attendant. Creusa, who has realized that Ion might be the real son she wants to find, is incensed when she hears what Xuthus has been told and tries to kill Ion. She fails and has to take refuge herself. A priestess then arrives with tokens that show Ion to be Creusa's child. The one missing piece of the jigsaw which would turn this into a standard new comedy plot is the information that it was Xuthus who happened to rape Creusa in the first place, *incognito*. A hundred years later Menander's *Arbitration* will have almost exactly this story line. But *Ion* is pure Euripides. Creusa does know who she was raped by and it certainly was not Xuthus. It was Apollo, and about that she is adamant. This casts a different light upon proceedings. Instead of an elementary comedy of manners, admittedly before its time, but still with all intrigue and misunderstanding resolved in the manner of the well-made play, we have instead a spirited and sceptical drama which examines, often in comic terms but with human nerves exposed, a variety of themes from responsibility for past actions to the dubious interference of the gods in men's affairs.

The more closely one looks at *Ion* the more apparent it becomes that one of the most potent ideas explored is how difficult it is to define the past by means of present action. If this sounds fanciful in a playwright of the fifth century BC, and rather more the province of a Beckett or a Pinter, consider only the method by which solutions to the play's problems are tried out and then discarded. The prologue has Hermes laying bare the outlines of the plot. Apollo raped Creusa. Creusa exposed Ion, complete with tokens, *chlide* (literally 'luxury' or 'adornment' of any kind). Apollo asked Hermes to preserve the child. Hermes deposited it on the steps of the temple. So much for the past. For the present Hermes reveals that Apollo will fix it for Xuthus to claim Ion as his own son.

The human beings then proceed to behave rather differently from the way the myth has ordained. Creusa is worried that Apollo may let it out that she has already had a child, for all that it is his own. Ion, when he hears from Creusa what happened to a 'friend' of hers, as she tells him, is so incensed he decides to confront Apollo with his viciousness. When Xuthus claims Ion as his son, he confesses to a youthful indiscretion and Ion accepts that he could be Xuthus' illegitimate son. The Chorus are not convinced: 'This oracle worries me in case it is a trick'. They then tell Creusa about Ion. She reacts with a tirade against Apollo and plots to kill Ion. At last there is the revelation by the priestess, who produces the cradle in which she says Ion was found, complete with swaddling clothes. When Ion examines the cradle he discovers it is miraculously new-looking, but Creusa is able to describe a piece of weaving inside and Ion at last accepts that Creusa is his mother. What he cannot believe is that Apollo is his father: 'Look, mother, did you not give way to a secret love-affair – girls do – and then blame it on a god?'. Creusa will make no such admission, but she does not convince Ion, who decides to force his way into the temple and demand the truth from Apollo. It is at that moment that Athene arrives, 'coming for Apollo who did not think it right to reveal himself to you'. She gives her version of events and decrees that Xuthus shall be kept in ignorance of the truth about the past, to keep him happy. And Ion at last accepts his mother's version of events.

By any kind of standards this is a weird moral tale. The series of reversals can be seen as perverse human reactions to the best-laid plans of gods and goddesses, but perhaps the complex chain of events has a more far-reaching purpose than to cast doubt on the neutrality of the Delphic oracle. We find, for example, further emphasis on the visual anomaly of the Periclean *skene*. The play proper opens with Ion sweeping the stage and chasing off with bow and arrows the birds which are attempting to build their nests in the temple cornices. The Chorus arrive like a group of tourists off the bus from Athens, admiring the friezes, in acknowledgement either of the elaborate scene-painting or as an ironic joke about the lack of it. That the Chorus should admire Delphi because its temple facade is as well decorated as one in Athens might even be a tribute to the precinct of Pericles, completed at last after so many years of building. What would be hard to accept is a chorus given all these specific references without a specific purpose.

Much the same could be said of the tokens which seem so miraculously new. The priestess, Ion and Creusa draw attention to these properties which become as much the centre of the scene as do the urn and bow in the *Electra* and *Philoctetes* of Sophocles. For that very reason the newness of the cradle is more than a minor refinement, while Creusa's ability to describe its contents in detail concentrates the audience on physical objects which they can take seriously and rely upon, even if humanity is so fickle.

It is perhaps here that the principal interest of this curious but compelling play resides. Interpretations, as of many revolutionary theatre pieces, are various and subtle, dependent, many of them, on either an intimate understanding of a sociological background, or upon some complex parochial argument, much of it no longer decipherable. Confined simply to its human reference and an established theatrical framework, *Ion* ceases to be either illogical or merely transitional between conflicting genres. It actually explores a stage world where humans react to fanciful events. In this it is precisely the same sort of comedy as the other plays discussed in this chapter. That it looks forward in plotline to new comedy is entirely fortuitous and not the play's *raison d'être*. What Euripides wrote for the audience to witness was comedy of contrast.

In *Cyclops* the comedy arises from grotesque reaction to potentially tragic event. *Alcestis* uses the boorishness of Heracles to point out the callousness of Admetus, so that the latter grows to sensitivity out of the revelation of the former's better nature. In *Iphigeneia in Tauris* we catch sight of real affection despite contrary circumstance, and the mellowness of *Helen* reasserts human and humane values. Here in *Ion* the mortal characters appear contrary, superficial and even murderous. The audience is unsure from one minute to the next where to place sympathy or whose word to rely on. As with the Chorus, who so much admire the set, but distrust the oracle, the various sentiments seem little more than a front.

Until, that is, the presentation of the tokens. The characters are reduced to basics. Creusa and Ion return to the point at which their relationship was first fractured. Through the tokens, fantastical as they seem, the characters can renew themselves, and begin to build. However ambivalent the position of Xuthus may seem to be, he is at least content with what he gets. The gods may not be infallible, but at least they retrieve one another's transgressions. Creusa and Ion find prosperity beyond the temporary setbacks within the play.

It is quite possible to dismiss Euripides simply as a cynic, and it is perhaps because of this that even in his happier plays critics have looked for the sour at the expense of the regenerative. Euripides' comedies are often serious, as the comedies of Aristophanes were often serious, but they are none the less comedies, whatever their festival definition. In this the comic touch offered a new dimension to the playwright's iconoclasm and afforded him the opportunity to explore the stage image in ever wider and more comprehensive a fashion.

Euripides and Sophocles both died in 405 BC. Three of the plays which survive were first produced posthumously. And there, as far as we are concerned, Greek tragedy draws to a close. The festivals continued. New tragedies were written, but by common consent, and Aristophanes in *Frogs* could see it coming, there was little that was original or worthy to be ranked with the works of the fifth-century masters. It may be that, as the theatre mirrors society, so the decline of tragedy reflected the passing of a golden age. Perhaps the stimulus to the tragedians was created only by the peculiar combination of political and social circumstances which saw the rise and fall of the Athenian empire. Or could it be that the approach to the presentation of plays in the tragic form was so comprehensively explored by Aeschylus, Sophocles and Euripides that the Athenian theatre could accommodate no further innovation, at least in the handling of serious matter?

Seneca aside, it took another two thousand years before tragedy acquired an alternative form. Tragedy is the product of new ages. When the vision of the individual succeeds in capturing a general mood and translating it into art, then that art becomes the most effective statement of its times. The Greek sense of theatre serves as a testament for classical Athens. It serves also as the basic standard against which all later tragedy, even Shakespearean, must be judged. This model value derives from the plays themselves and from the play-wrights, but it is centred in a communal artistic and spiritual achievement which enshrined the experience of the entire audience. What Aeschylus, Sophocles and Euripides perfected was the basic grammar of the theatre.

EPILOGUE

An epilogue should either be a pithy and concise summary on the old essay principle that you should say what you are going to say, say it and then say that you have said it, or a valedictory speech in verse from the protagonist asking for the audience's goodwill. This is neither, though perhaps a little bit of both. It is a plea for all the plays of the Greek tragic theatre to be regarded as worthy of the attention of our major theatrical spirits, in the same way as are the plays of Shakespeare: Greek tragedy as a corpus, rather than as a corpse.

From the time of the Restoration, Shakespeare's plays in revival have always been a part of the staple diet of our theatres. The more bizarre aberrations of some periods leave us today amazed at the sensibilities that perpetrated them. But if *Macbeths* full of dancing witches and *King Lears* with happy endings are as little to our modern taste as we assume they would have been to Shakespeare's, we must applaud the desire of every age to keep the plays on the stage. Shakespeare was not always the winner, but he survives.

'The classics, it seems to me, have to be rediscovered every ten years or so. The traditional elements must be appreciated and handed on; at the same time the actor must somehow contribute a contemporary approach from within.' So wrote Sir John Gielgud. But when he refers to 'the classics' he means

Shakespeare, he means Farquhar perhaps, Sheridan, Ibsen, Chekhov, Shaw. He does not mean Aeschylus, Sophocles, Euripides and Aristophanes.

Oliver Taplin concludes his *Greek Tragedy in Action*, an admirable statement of the case for the Greek plays as stage pieces, with a chapter on 'Round plays in square theatres' in which he applauds classical production: '. . .during the last hundred years there has been a huge revival in the staging of Greek tragedy after a lapse of some 1500 years.'[1] While commending his optimism, I have to take issue with his description of the revival as 'huge'. It seems to me paltry, at least at a professional level, when set against the size of the potential repertoire and the comparative popularity of the drama of the Renaissance. Some commendable efforts at Greenwich and the Mermaid apart, the number of major productions of classical Greek tragedies seen in our professional theatres in the last forty years can be counted on two hands.

But why should that be? Greek plays still have a performance tradition, albeit a slightly stolid one, in their native Greece. Do they not travel well? Shakespeare has managed to be popular in Russia, China and South America despite translation difficulties. Perhaps it is the plots and characters of Greek drama, based on myth. And yet the attitude of the European theatre to the classical tragedies has largely been to accept Greek myth and convert it into prime material for original works. In our own century we need only point to Stravinsky, Martha Graham, Sartre, Cocteau, O'Neill and all those tedious Eliot plays. No, the plots and characters have inspired other theatre practitioners for better, or, more often, for worse.

I can only assume that there is something about the plays themselves which has frightened off the great directors. There have been revivals, of course: an *Oresteia* and an *Oedipus Rex* from Reinhardt, another *Oedipus Rex* from Guthrie, an *Antigone* from Tairov and a version from Brecht, a *Medea* from Oklopkhov. But how can it have happened that those very directors most equipped to exploit the mask, Meyerhold, Copeau, George Devine and Peter Brook, ignored a set of plays written for masked performance?

Within the last few years the Royal Shakespeare Company

1 *Greek Tragedy in Action*, London, Methuen, 1978, p. 172.

and the National Theatre Company have tried to restore the balance. The results have been variable. For the Royal Shakespeare Company John Barton produced *The Greeks*, a cycle culled from all three tragedians with one of his own thrown in. He presented them as a sequence, as though they told a single story and the Agamemnons, the Helens and Electras of any two plays were meant to be the same character. The Electra plays alone show how misleading such a premise must be. Euripides could choose to write an *Orestes* as well as an *Electra* because characterization was one of the variables of Greek tragedy. People could be redrawn even if the circumstances were largely given.

The National Theatre Company, one of whose aims and duties is to foster the world's repertoire, had an early and undistinguished foray into Sophocles with *Philoctetes* (revived more recently at the Manchester Royal Exchange), a flirtation with the *Bacchae* in a free adaptation by the Nigerian playwright Wole Soyinka, and, most recently, a full-scale masked *Oresteia* directed by Sir Peter Hall. The translation by Tony Harrison represents a considerable feat of imaginative composition, but in production sound dominated sight, and the mask was the loser. The positive aspects of these productions were considerable but both *The Greeks* and the *Oresteia* must be chalked up as opportunities missed.

It is all too easy in the light of this book to assign the shortcomings of such productions to a devotion to the spoken word. To do so would be to over-simplify. But what does seem to have been absent from both *The Greeks* and the *Oresteia* is the spirit of the originals, that quality which made the performances in Athens an experience for the emotions as well as the mind, the quality that Aristotle set out to justify after it had so frightened Plato. It was this which ensured that the Theatre of Dionysus was crammed from morning till night for three days running to see those first productions. That spirit was far more than mere language.

There are some encouraging signs. In Berlin Peter Stein returned for his *Antiquity Project* to the original concerns of the Greek theatre and applied his own sense of theatrecraft to the essentials he discovered. In *Gospel at Colonnus* Lee Breuer improbably transferred Sophocles into the milieu of black gospel music, and with surprising success. All it needs is a proper realization of what the dramatist prescribed in the first place and the vision to translate this into terms a contemporary audience can appreciate. The themes can never have seemed more topical: warmongering in the guise of patriotism, demagoguery of the right and the left, the virtues and dangers of individualism, the rule of law and those who set themselves above it in the name of rank or cause. They could hardly be more immediate. And there are the perennial themes, the ones that Shakespeare explored as well: the responsibilities of kinship and friendship, the assertion of spiritual values and the search, in the face of the most overwhelming odds, for compassion.

There is no reason why the plays of the Greek tragedians should not appear as regularly on our modern stage as those from any other period of major theatrical enterprise. These tragedies are as amenable to the 'rediscovery' that Gielgud talks of, as any other classics – and not just the familiar few. There should be a regular place on our stages for a *Prometheus*, a *Women of Trachis*, for *Alcestis*, *Madness of Heracles*, *Ion* and a host of others. They all derive from the vision of a generation of playwrights who, it is claimed, created the European tradition. The proper test of such a claim is on a stage where the performance values which ensured their first success can be revitalized with something of their original drive.

INDEX

Bold type indicates a special emphasis.